Not Ready to Walk Alone

Not Ready to Walk Alone

Judith Fabisch

ZONDERVAN PUBLISHING HOUSE
OF THE ZONDERVAN CORPORATION
GRAND RAPIDS, MICHIGAN 49506

NOT READY TO WALK ALONE
Copyright © 1978 by The Zondervan Corporation
Grand Rapids, Michigan

Library of Congress Cataloging in Publication Data

Fabisch, Judith.
    Not ready to walk alone.

    Bibliography: p.
    1.   Fabisch, Judith.   2.   Widows—United States
—Biography.   3.   Christian biography—United
States.   4.   Consolation.   I.   Title.
BV4908.F32   248'.86 [B]   78-6724
ISBN 0-310-37070-1

PRINTED IN THE UNITED STATES OF AMERICA

For Ed and Diane Fuller,
who cared,
and for Scott,
my constant delight

Contents

Preface

Widowhood is not an easy calling, and I seemed little prepared to meet the challenges that its imposition would present. God had plans for me, however, that included areas of personal growth I had never envisioned.

March 18, 1973, dawned early with the realization that my husband, who lay beside me, the man with whom I had laughed and cried and loved for almost fifteen years, was breathing his last. Even before reaching the hospital to hear the solemn edict, "Your husband has succumbed," the Lord had enclosed me in a circle of love and comfort that was to be my constant stay throughout the days and months and years ahead.

I made a lot of mistakes, but those mistakes were learning experiences, and I feel it is a great privilege to be able to share that knowledge with others. There have been wonderful victories, too, and the knowledge of the Source of those victories is an even greater blessing to share. Some of the examples on the following pages are mine, but certainly not all of them. They have been accumulated from association with many others who have shared the experience of widowhood. Not all have been happy, but without exception they are true. The names and details have been changed slightly so there will be no reflection on the actual persons involved.

There are so many people to thank. Without the assistance of Dr. Raymond Bartholomew, who encouraged, advised, and gave many more hours than I could reasonably expect, the manuscript would never have been prepared. Dr. Ronald Chadwick offered the initial challenge, and without his enthusiasm I doubt that I would have had the courage to begin. Mrs. Darlaine Gates offered consistent prayer support, and for that she deserves special gratitude.

The paths my feet have walked in the five years since Ed's death have been so far from their original course, and the blessings received have been so great there is little doubt in my mind that this has clearly been "God's better plan" for me. Standing in the afterglow of the love shared by my husband and myself, I still must raise my most grateful thanks to the Lord who brought all of these things to pass.

> Blessed be God, even the Father of our Lord Jesus Christ, the Father of mercies, and the God of all comfort; Who comforteth us in all our tribulation that we may be able to comfort them which are in any trouble, by the comfort wherewith we ourselves are comforted of God
> (2 Cor. 1:3-4).

Does Jesus Care?

Does Jesus care when my heart is pained
Too deeply for mirth and song?
As the burdens press, and the cares distress
And the way grows weary and long?

Does Jesus care when my way is dark
With a nameless dread and fear?
As the daylight fades into deep night shades,
Does He care enough to be near?

Does Jesus care when I've tried and failed
To resist some temptation strong
When for my deep grief I find no relief,
Tho' my tears flow all the night long?

Does Jesus care when I've said "good-by"
To the dearest on earth to me,
And my sad heart aches till it nearly breaks
Is it aught to Him? Does He see?

Oh yes, He cares, I know He cares,
His heart is touched with my grief;
When the days are weary, the long nights
   dreary, I know my Savior cares.

—Frank E. Graeff

Three Out of Four

CHAPTER ONE

Three Out of Four

It happens in many ways—the screech of brakes and the crunching of metal; or an early morning drama of rasping breath, frantic phone calls, and flashing ambulance lights; or the quiet proclamation by a solemn-faced physician that the pain is at long last ended. However it happens, you're never quite ready for the "till death do us part"—not ready for his life to become a number, listed in neat little columns by the Bureau of Statistics—not ready to end the relationship so carefully nurtured by you both—not ready to walk alone.

"Widow" conjures up in the minds of most a line of elderly ladies with snow-white hair, quiet and proper, sitting near the front of the church. Faces change now and then (add a few, remove a few) of these harmless little ladies who complain vaguely about loneliness and arthritis, occasionally, when someone remembers to ask. How poorly we have perceived their needs and dismissed the thought of them with, "I sure hope I never get like that."

If the widow is a member of a younger generation, we change our reaction only slightly: we "tsk" sadly, and the phrase that locks the door of further consideration becomes, "I don't know how she does it! I know I couldn't." Somehow, the admission of unpreparedness for the widowed state seems to remove the probability for the necessity of it.

The appalling problems spawned by this attitude are as numerous as the women they affect. Cold, hard statistics indicate that, sooner or later, widowhood will be the status of nearly three-fourths of all women who marry.[1] At all ages, among all races, and independent of the state of preparedness, wives outlive their husbands. These women are thrust abruptly into a life style which, for the most part, they are neither prepared for nor desire.

The consequences of their unpreparedness are a shocking testimony of the unrealistic attitudes held by so many. Women may flock to Thursday morning classes in cake decorating. The art of macramé has engaged both young and old in spirited searches for exactly the right twine and involved them in lengthy discussions concerning the art of knot-tying. Many a relaxing morning is spent by women deciding on "just the right shade of blue" for the paint-it-yourself ceramics that have become the current rage. These same women, however, may have no idea of how to balance a checkbook. They don't know what kind of insurance their husbands have, or with what companies. The operation of the power lawnmower is a deep mystery to them, one they do not care to solve. In short, in their estimation, household maintenance consists of weekly

---

[1]U.S. Department of Commerce, Bureau of the Census, *Statistical Abstract of the United States, 1975*, p. 38.

cleaning and keeping the grocery bill within the limits of hubby's temper. The examples are legion.

Still in the shock of disbelief over the news of her husband's accidental death, Marcie, age 29, was surrounded by relatives and fed tranquilizers until reality became a hazy fog. Addiction to barbituate use became a real threat. For more than a month after the funeral she was literally not allowed to think or act for herself. Others planned the funeral, of which she has only a dim recollection. Others shared her bed. Others cooked her meals and cared for her children.

When presented with the need to consider the alternatives of workmen's compensation insurance, the pressure from relatives to "take all you can get right now" prompted her to opt for increased benefits for a period of seven years, regardless of her future marital state. She rejected a reduced benefit, which would terminate only in the event of her remarriage.

Her boys will be only fourteen and fifteen years of age when this supplement to her inadequate social security payments expires. In addition, when her boys reach the age of eighteen, all of her own social security benefits will terminate until she herself reaches retirement age.

What could have provided a cushion of security for the years when she might not be able to work will be unavailable to her because she was totally unprepared to make the decision. In choosing a temporary steak-for-hamburger existence, she may well settle for peanut butter in the days to come.

In retrospect, she realizes that if she does remarry, the dollar gain is of comparatively minor importance. However, the fact of the decision stands, and there remain bitter feelings of "being pushed" at a time when she was not even capable of deciding what to make for dinner. Had she and her husband considered the alternatives prior to his death, the outcome might have been quite different. Knowing the attitudes of relatives, counsel from him beforehand might have given her the courage to turn away the unwelcome houseguests and tranquilizers and more quickly resume control of her own life.

Had the financial situation been realistically discussed, the decision would almost certainly have been a different one.

Although financial security was not a problem for Irma, retirement-aged, she had so completely blocked the possibility of her husband preceding her in death that when news of it came to her, she reacted with physical and mental shock. Her hospitalization for several weeks prevented her attendance at the funeral, which had to be planned by her adult children. It was months before she was able to carry on a relevant conversation, and she was forced to retire from leadership of a women's organization she had previously enjoyed. Her inability to care for herself and her home made rebuilding a life for herself a tedious and frustrating process. Since she was unable to mow the lawn or make simple household repairs, the house became an eyesore. When her washing machine broke, she carried her laundry to a laundromat for several months because she "didn't know whom to call." Only the chance discovery of the situation by a friend alleviated her problem.

Some widows choose to "adjust" by ignoring the real world and creating one of their own—especially those who do not have to seek employment for financial survival. Alice, age 45, lost her orientation to time. She gradually worked into a schedule of staying up into the small hours of the morning to watch television, and then slept through the greater part of the day. Regular meals became an unknown commodity, contacts with the outside world were seriously curtailed, and she frequently remained clothed in only her robe and nightgown for days at a time. Alcohol became an ever-increasing factor in her life, and only when her own teen-aged children rebelled against her lack of concern for them by rejecting her did she make any attempt at change. Unfortunately, it was too late to restore the previous relationship. Although both her son and daughter live within the same city as their mother, telephone calls or visits must always be initiated by her. They are so painful as to be risked only on a yearly basis. Consolation for Alice came in reverting back to the behavior that caused the problem. Her bitterness has turned away so many from her door that if she were to die, discovery might well depend on the length of the grass in her lawn.

In contrast to Alice, Irene escaped the reality of the loss of her husband by holding close her remaining unmarried son. He deeply resented the denial of the same carefree life his older brothers had experienced. Instead of automobiles, parties, and girl friends, his lot seemed to be a never-ending series of household chores, errands, and shopping trips with his mother. She encouraged the immediate expenditure of any money he earned so he would not be able to purchase an automobile when he came of age. The resentments thus built up finally exploded when he brought home the girl he intended to marry. Irene's opposition was so intense that the son took his bride in spite of the objection and moved to another city. The adjustments to practical matters of household repair, automobile maintenance, and out-of-town driving, which should have been faced at her husband's death, now loomed large before her. She eventually gained the necessary skills and confidence, but the alienation between mother and son remains.

LIKE it or not, relatives are often the primary source of frustration. Frank discussion of potential problems before-the-fact can eliminate a great deal of heartache. Human nature being what it is, close relationships forming immediately after the funeral, holding forth much sympathy and understanding, often should be suspect of ulterior motives. Too many of these friendships last just as long as the free handouts. Of course, it isn't practical (or even healthy) to discuss the disposition of every item brought into the home in the event of death, but realistically discussing personalities that may be involved can greatly aid in approaching the subject with a degree of intelligence, should such disposition be necessary.

Joan's in-laws were of great comfort to her immediately

after her husband's death. Weekly or semi-weekly visits by his brothers from a distance of some fifty miles were most welcome. Each seemed happy to lend a helping hand for almost any chore she could not handle herself—including the cleaning of the basement. Grateful, Joan urged them to share her husband's sporting equipment. Fishing tackle, boots, camp stoves, rifles, handguns, snow-sport equipment, and clothing disappeared into the automobiles of their new owners. The next "semi-weekly" visit occurred some four months later, when Joan made a holiday "command performance" at Grandma's house, and on that occasion it proved necessary for one of the brothers to depart early—to make use of his newly acquired means of relaxation.

Another area that seems to breed more bitterness than love is the sale of major items to relatives. An automobile, boat, motor, or any other item which performs with less than perfection can be "that lemon you sold me," a source of bitterness far exceeding the advantages of an easy sale. The discovery that an item was sold below the actual market value can be the thorn in the flesh that grows into the wedge of family division. Helen, finding herself in possession of two cars at the time of her husband's death, agreed to sell the smaller one, in need of repair, to her married son. The sale price was dealer value, not market value, a fact overlooked by both of the parties concerned. After repairing the automobile, he sold it at a substantial profit, and purchased the vehicle that he had wanted all along. The remaining auto, unfortunately, was far too large for Helen's driving abilities or needs. Before long it was punctuated with a series of indentations from ill-executed turns. Rusting and an eyesore, there are no funds for replacement. Annual visits between the two are brief and cool, with superficiality the only apparent alternative to explosion.

The tragedies of psychological adjustment are heartrending, but sadder still are the instances of those who are in real material need. In the vast majority of cases, social security is sadly inadequate, and the women receiving these inadequate funds are just as sadly lacking in marketable skills. The benefit received by a widow is based on the average of her husband's lifetime earnings (the low as well as the high). An average monthly earning of about $425 receives a benefit of less than $225 per month—scarcely enough to pay the rent in many areas. (A chart included at the end of chapter 4 shows some typical benefits received.) With children, and consideration of the age at death, this amount could be somewhat larger, but the maintenance of a household on social security funds is a far-fetched dream that only the very fortunate ever realize. The girl who barely paused long enough to change clothes between high-school graduation and the wedding ceremony is scarcely equipped to earn a living that will support herself and her dependent children. College graduation is no guarantee either—a degree in the humanities equips one for little more than the receipt of cap, gown, and signed diploma. Too often these women are found seeking public assistance or "slinging hash" in a restaurant for a mere pittance in order to keep house and home together.

When her husband insisted on purchasing life insurance, Shelly hurried out of the room, declaring that insurance was "men's business, and really not all that necessary anyway." His meager salary allowed for only $10,000 of coverage, but his intentions were to increase the amount as soon as possible. Before he could act upon his intentions, however, he died, and the unscrupulous agent who delivered the check to Shelly promptly sold her a $25,000 paid-up life insurance policy—at a price of $10,000, the exact amount of her benefit! While the small amount would not have provided a living for her, to be sure, it would have given her something to fall back on in the event of illness or other emergency. Invested wisely, with accruing interest, it would have been an excellent source of funds for the education of her two children. Unfortunately, her reserve is now invested in a way that will not be profitably recoverable for many years. Though the action of this agent is unethical by any standards, he is certainly only one of an army, eager to capitalize on the naiveté of one inexperienced in financial matters.

The nest egg that is so carefully saved by many couples to help them through in times of trouble is often eaten away by the expenses involved with a final illness or in funeral expenses. Not only is the understanding undertaker anxious to help the widow obtain the very best, but cemetery plots in the price range of $1,500 are not at all unusual. Add to those costs that of a grave marker (a modest one is often priced near $300), and the nest egg must be sizeable indeed to cover even the bare minimums.

Plans made "before the fact" can save untold anxiety and dollars. Social security has a burial allowance of less than $250, and only the barest of funerals will fall within that price range. However, the $3,000 expense so easily incurred (without cemetery lot and grave marker) is often nothing more than an emotional decision.

THE best preparation for widowhood begins on the wedding day. An overprotective husband may flatter his bride, but he does her no favor. Very little gratitude will be felt when the basement floor is four inches deep with water and the widow doesn't know how to trigger the sump pump. Nor would his children appreciate the death-dealing shock delivered to their mother should she approach this situation improperly.

The bride may feel pampered and loved when her husband tends dutifully to the furnace, but the widow only feels cold when she doesn't know how to operate the switch that turns the furnace from summer to winter operation. A practical lesson on the operation of the snowblower may be chilling, but it is infinitely easier than the anguish experienced when a child is suffering from pains suggestive of appendicitis, and the driveway is still blocked with eight inches of snow.

A young wife may feel relieved that she doesn't have to bother her head about financial matters, but her anxiety will be multiplied if she doesn't know how or where to make the house payment. Never having to change a flat tire may save a new manicure, but it can be ruin to the already strained budget of the widow if she has to call professional assistance to do the job for her.

The widow *will* make a new life for herself, but the quality of that life depends to a great degree on her preparedness to meet it and deal with the challenges it presents. Not that widowhood will ever be easy—the world of the half-married is strewn with obstacles of responsibility and loneliness that only the most insensitive would deny. But, in learning to deal with the problems that arise in a practical, common-sense manner, she opens the way for personal growth and maturity that her married sister cannot appreciate.

Just as swimming lessons prove their worth only when the boat tips over, so can preparedness ease the confusion often brought on when a woman finds herself in the strange new world called widowhood.

Cry, and You
Cry Alone

CHAPTER TWO

Cry, and You Cry Alone

When the boat has tipped is a poor time to think about swimming lessons. This is the approach used, however, by many women toward the possibility of widowhood. Once "in the water" they flail about helplessly, grasping at every floating twig or leaf in an effort to buoy themselves up. Face-to-face with reality, they find themselves alone, confused, and frightened, able only to wail at their plight.

Grief is common, and the reality of grief is faced, almost without exception, by the vast majority of adults. How they face their loss depends to a great extent upon the focus of their lives. The woman who visits her husband's grave on a daily basis, offering up tears and flowers to his memory, deceives no one but herself into believing that he was and still is all she ever lived for. She might just as well admit to herself and the world that she is simply too self-centered to want to face life alone and that she feels very sorry for herself. For a while, friends and relatives may sympathize with her and tolerate such behavior, but before long they will tire of such uncomfortable circumstances and turn away from the scene. Her narrow range of conversational topics, her continual grieving attitude, her one focus of life, like drug addiction, decreases her circle of relationships until there is no one left but herself and the silent grave she visits. She is alone in the water, and the night is very dark.

As widows we may feel perfectly justified in our grief. The loss we have suffered is very real—none will deny it, and our feelings have many precedents. When King David's son Absalom revolted against him and threatened to take away his kingdom, David's enduring love for his wayward son was expressed in his words to the departing warriors, "Deal gently for my sake with the young man, even with Absalom." Despite this caution, Absalom was killed, and David's grief is heart-rending. The pathetic agony of his cry, "O my son Absalom, O Absalom, my son, my son," reaches across the ages to all those who have lost someone dear. David's grief was completely self-centered, however. He ignored almost completely the multitude of his subjects who had risked their lives so that he could retain his throne, the throne that would someday belong to his son Solomon, by God's decree. By his tears and wailing he so much as told them that their lives were not important, that their sacrifice was not significant. Nothing mattered to him except the fact that he had lost his son.

GRIEF is not wrong. It is a necessary step in the healing of the emotions, and to ignore it places the whole process of recovery in jeopardy. When a bad seam has been sewn in a garment, the way to correct it is not to hastily tear the pieces of cloth apart; to do so might cause the whole garment to be ruined. Instead, the stitches are removed carefully—sometimes one at a time—so that the cloth will remain sound and able to be used again.

To feel no sorrow at the departure of a loved one either puts a small price on the relationship or denies an essential process that will be paid for in "damaged cloth" at a later date. To allow grief to degenerate into self-pity, however, denies the very love of God. It refuses to even touch the stitches. A child taken out of one school and placed in another often doesn't see that the change is for his own good. Rather he mourns old friends and teachers and loses any benefits he might have gained, not counting that his parents acted in love. And so, the widow must see that God is always acting in love, no matter what the outward appearance of His acts may seem.

We are also shown another response of David, in an experience prior to Absolom's death, when that great king of Israel was living in right relationship to God. Having admitted his guilt in the matter of Bathsheba and Uriah, he saw that his sin was foremost a sin against God. Repentant and forgiven, the consequences had still to be borne. The child who had come forth from that illicit union would die. David's sorrow was grievous while the child lay ill, and when it died his servants trembled to bring him the news. As David questioned his whispering servants and found that his fasting and prayer had been in vain, his response was a total shock to them:

> Then David arose from the earth, and washed, and anointed himself, and changed his apparel, and came into the house of the LORD, and worshipped: then he came to his own house; and when he required, they set bread before him, and he did eat. . . . And he said, While the child was yet alive, I fasted and wept: for I said, Who can tell whether God will be gracious to me, that the child may live? . . . And David comforted Bathsheba his wife, and went in unto her . . . (2 Sam. 12:20,22,24a).

In contrast to the incident involving Absalom's death, here David's life was totally God-centered. He had borne a loss, and that loss had a heavy burden of guilt associated with it. The difference in David's reaction here and his reaction to Absalom's death was that in this instance David said, in effect, "Yes, God." Here, David was acknowledging God's perfect ways. He was concerned with the lives and emotions of others, not merely with his own personal feelings. He did not ignore what had happened; he accepted it.

"Yes, God" doesn't change the facts. Death is death, and mere assent or denial of God's will does not alter reality. What does change is our attitude toward that reality; acceptance instead of rebellion; being God-centered rather than self-centered. With some of us, the problem is that we want to remain objects of pity, no matter what our outer (or inner) protestations to such an accusation. We want to feel sorry for ourselves. When the sympathy and the flowers pass away, we feel offended. Only as we enter into a proper relationship to God are we able to respond to grief with an outward look, away from ourselves.

Just as David's problem was sin, so is ours, and likewise the problem of all mankind. There is not one person on the face of the earth that has ever, of himself, lived in right relationship to God. God's verdict is clear, "There is none righteous, no, not one" (Rom. 3:10). We may deceive ourselves temporarily into thinking that we have led good lives, or that we have led better lives than our neighbor; but one must shout long and loud indeed to muffle the voice of conscience that knows better than to believe one is without blame, and the absence of blame is the requirement. God's holiness is the standard, and we can no more hope to meet it than we can hope to fill the Grand Canyon with water from a teaspoon.

"All have sinned and come short of the glory of God" (Rom. 3:23). Not one of us has met the standard. The wages of such falling short have long been established. God declared them to Adam and Eve when He placed the tree of the knowledge of good and evil "off-limits," and that wage has not changed through all the ages: "The wages of sin is death . . ." (Rom. 6:23). Physical death is only one side of the problem, and

30

as tragic as that side is, it is the lesser of importance. The greater tragedy is the spiritual death that accompanies such payment. Physical death is a temporary state, but those who would remain spiritually dead in this life will find no consolation in eternity.

We can't spoon righteousness as we can water, but fortunately, God has made provision for us that we could never make for ourselves. "God commended his love toward us, in that, while we were yet sinners, Christ died for us" (Rom. 5:8). In Christ, God has resolved the problem of spiritual death that faces all of us, and it is for us to appropriate the benefits of that provision. Mere assent to the facts is not enough. James tells us, ". . . the devils also believe, and tremble" (James 2:19). What is necessary is faith that those facts are relevant to one's personal life. "There is therefore now no condemnation to them which are in Christ Jesus" (Rom. 8:1). Faith that is saving faith will result in new attitudes toward sin, new attitudes toward God, and new attitudes toward His Word, the Bible. Thankfulness will spring spontaneously from a heart grateful for a secure future—not because of instruction or example, but because of overwhelming love for One who did so much in the face of our total unworthiness.

Salvation is a personal relationship with Jesus Christ, one which benefits not only in eternity, but in the here-and-now. Without that relationship to Christ the widow is cast adrift on a lonely sea of confusion. Deprived of the companionship and counsel of the one with whom she intended to spend the rest of her days, she finds herself bewildered by conflicting advice, lonely beyond measure, frustrated with problems she has no idea how to deal with, and angry that so much is now demanded of her. One needs read only a few of the secular sources on widowhood to realize that even the best adjustments without Christ often lead to bitterness and further misery. Not by any stretch of the imagination does this deny the presence of problems in the God-centered life, but the God-centered solutions to those problems are infinitely easier than the man-centered solutions we are capable of producing by ourselves.

GOD sometimes sends a drastic change into our lives because that change will enable us to come to a fuller realization of what He desires us to be. It might be that this will be the means to our personal salvation as we face, for the first time, our relationship with Him. It might be that He desires to bring enrichment into our lives that could not otherwise be achieved had He not forcefully extracted us from the place where we found our greatest security. When we finally come to the point of letting go, letting God have His way, with no objections or cries of self-pity, many problems disappear of themselves. Often, however, even the Christian becomes so egocentric in her approach that one can hardly tell her reaction from the one who has not experienced the blessings of salvation. We forget that God's plan transcends the realm of the temporal, and that His purpose is to conform us to the image of His Son. All is for our eternal good, even our widowhood. If He could have accomplished His purpose in our lives in any other way, any easier way, He would have.

The outward look, the God-centered look, does not insist on running back to the security of sameness, but realizes the opportunity for personal and spiritual growth. The God-centered look does not brood over grief like a mother hen over her chicks, but sees the consequence of widowhood, or any other of the trials that are part of the Christian life, as opportunity. The view is not merely survival, but the expression of a lively, healthy faith in a God who makes no mistakes, a God to whom we have committed the responsibility for our temporal and eternal well-being. We need not question each step of the way, need not know the reason why. If we simply trust that He knows the plan, there is no reason to fear; we will not be lost along the way. If we trust Him for our eternity, is it not foolish to be worried about today?

The God-centered look does not insist, "I cannot give up

my grieving," for that phrase all too often simply means, "I *won't* give up my grieving." Only as we find something or Someone of greater importance than our personal heartbreak will we ever gain victory over it. When we decide what is important to us, it is amazing what obstacles can be overcome. We've all heard stories of mothers who have rushed fearlessly into fires to rescue trapped children, or who have displayed Herculean strength to lift heavy objects holding loved ones from freedom. When God is the all-important figure, when His glory is the ultimate goal of our lives, then the results will be, likewise, noteworthy.

To be in right relationship with God brings with it immediate promises. Not only can the widow claim all that is offered to other believers, but she can be sure that God has noted her special circumstance. Not only is her God the God of Abraham and Isaac and Jacob, but her God is the God of Ruth and the widow of Zarephath and the widow of Nain. More than eighty references in Scripture concern either the welfare of the widow or that of her fatherless children.

The widow, fatherless, and sojourner were entitled, along with the Levite, to a portion of the triennial tithe and a portion of the offerings at feasts. Farmers were forbidden to harvest their fields completely so that those who were in need could avail themselves of the provision. One of the causes of Israel's captivity was the fact that the widow and the fatherless had been neglected.

Elijah's need at Zarephath was met by a widow of God's choosing, not a nice, elderly retired couple who couldn't make it on social security, or those cute newlyweds who were having trouble making ends meet on his meager salary, but a widow, who without God's help had to face starvation. Elisha helped to meet the need of the widow facing the sale of her sons into slavery by making sure that every pot she could find would be filled with oil for her to sell. In the New Testament, the marital status of Dorcas is not mentioned, but it was her ministry to make clothing for widows, and it was they who stood weeping for her at her death, and they who rejoiced at her restoration.

Modern-day widows may cry, "That was fine in the early days of Israel, and it was great that the widow of Zarephath didn't have to starve. The friends of Dorcas must have been glad to see her again, but I haven't received a portion of any triennial tithe lately, and the car payment is due tomorrow. Elijah hasn't passed this way in years, and so I guess it's oatmeal again tonight. The last time somebody gave me a garment, it was a coat so moth-eaten that I had to store it in a plastic bag until the garbage men came, for fear the rest of my clothing would be infested."

That may well be, but God does not change, and he is not limited by Elijah, Elisha, or Dorcas. He doesn't need help to fill the oil pots. The God who cared for widows in Bible times is the same God who cares for widows today. Those who feel they must bewail their plight might well seek the answers as to the source of their misery in other places. Are all the avenues of God's provision being used? Has pride prevented employment in a job that seems too demeaning? Has pride prevented asking for help? Are the things lacking really necessities, or are they merely desires? Paul says in Philippians 4:19, "But my God shall supply all your *need* according to his riches in glory by Christ Jesus." Perhaps there is a valuable lesson to be learned, and by our whining and complaining we have closed the avenues of communication and are unable to profit by it.

Widowhood is an opportunity not only for the discovery of God's sufficiency, but for the proclamation of that fact. It affords avenues, as never before, to show forth the beauty of Christ to a watching world. All eyes are watching—most are afraid. Death frightens people who have not met the Savior. From the overzealous tombstone salesman who approaches you the day after the funeral, to the funeral director himself, to the neighbor who is afraid to tell her husband what happened to yours because he has the same condition, you have a captive audience. They will listen now, as never before.

Here is, perhaps, the greatest test of the reality of one's

faith. The curtains are pulled back; there is no pretending—at least not for long. What *is* your attitude toward death? What *is* your attitude about God's control of your life? Do you *really* believe that "to die is gain" (Phil. 1:21)? Do you *really* believe that all things work together to conform us to the image of His Son (Rom. 8:28)? Or do you resent God for allowing this to happen to you?

IF THERE is one attitude more destructive than self-pity, it is guilt. It raises its ugly head under many guises. "If I hadn't sent him to the store," "If we hadn't argued," "If I hadn't been so stubborn," and a thousand more "ifs" are probably responsible for more guilty feelings than all of the revolvers ever manufactured.

The first thing to remember is that we don't control human life or circumstances—God does. Our thoughts do not determine a man's end. No matter what the argument or errand or attitude, we must agree with the truth that Job discovered long ago, ". . . the Lord gave, and the Lord hath taken away." The guilt we assume is Satan's tool to destroy our testimony of victorious Christian living. The argument which ends in a heart attack may or may not have been the fault of the now-grieving wife, but the heart attack itself was allowed by God. The trip to the store which ended in a fatal accident may have been an errand missed by a forgetful wife, but the accident could not have taken place without divine permission.

Secondly, Christ died so that we could be free of our burden of guilt. However we blame ourselves for the death of a mate, "If we confess our sins, he is faithful and just to forgive us our sins, and to cleanse us from all unrighteousness" (1 John 1:9). If we have confessed all of our fault in the matter and are truly repentant, all remaining guilt is false.

The choice is a personal one. Just as when we have a dress that is too long, we can either wear it as it is and look dowdy, or learn to hem that dress and be free from such embarrassment; so we can confess and believe that forgiveness has been granted as God has promised, or we can spend the rest of our lives chained to defeat.

Widowhood is a burden too heavy to be borne alone, and God never intended that we should do so; but only as we look to Christ and apply His finished work to our lives do we find the help we need.

Parting Is Not · Sweet Sorrow

CHAPTER THREE

Parting Is Not Sweet Sorrow

The first decisions of widowhood are financial and emotional and they must be made immediately. The reality of death has scarcely had time to penetrate; the time has not yet really come to miss him, for he might well still be at work, or at the board meeting, or running the errands he had listed for this afternoon. And yet, here is a funeral director and caskets and talk of flowers. The woman who may never have spent more than ten dollars without first consulting her husband is now faced with making a major expenditure under severe emotional stress, in many cases without realistic knowledge of the available resources.

Funeral costs range from several hundred dollars to several thousand. In some instances the price of the casket determines the total cost of the funeral. In other instances, each factor in the funeral is carefully itemized. Decisions must be made about vaults, cemetery lots, crypts, and perpetual care. "Economy," "Modest," and "Deluxe," become symbols of esteem, and genuine brass handles seem to be the only decent thing to provide. The confusion becomes more than one person can handle at a time like this, and she soon finds herself nodding yes to every suggestion made by friends, relatives, and the funeral director.

The ideal solution to this problem is to decide beforehand what is to be done and put it in writing in a will. If a couple agrees to the simplicity of cloth-covered wooden caskets, inexpensive cemetery lots, and a minimum of flowers, it becomes a simple matter to decide the details when the time is at hand. The objections of irate relatives are very simply countered when one can state, "This is the way it is written in his will."

If the quiet, simple funeral has not been decided on prior to death, it takes a great deal more courage than most of us possess to make that decision at the time the funeral is being ordered. If the widow can be accompanied by a person who is capable of tempering her emotional decisions somewhat, the cost factor can be controlled to some degree. Those who travel with widows to funeral parlors, however, are usually quite emotionally involved themselves, and such a find would be fortunate indeed.

It will make little difference to the deceased if the casket is bronze, hand-rubbed walnut, or pine. If the handles are genuine brass or merely grooves in the wood, there will be no protest raised from the grave. Many a man is buried surrounded by finer wood than any of the furniture he used during his lifetime, and he will never appreciate the difference.

A vault is required by many states, and the widow may or may not be shown a variety of them. They range in price from about $200 to $400, and their only purpose is to house the casket underground. All vaults sold meet state requirements, and the expenditure of extra money for polished surfaces and ten-year guarantees is vanity that can be ill-afforded by most families.

A cemetery lot or crypt is another major expenditure. Pine trees, willow trees, and a clear view through to the lake may be pleasant thoughts indeed. A crypt in "The Chapel of the Archangels" with piped-in music and air conditioning running through each individual chamber sounds romantic enough to bring sentimental tears to the eyes of even the most hard-hearted. Nonetheless, the widow's place is with the living, not the dead, and while there is nothing wrong with a few flowers on occasion, the gravesite is certainly not the place to visit to enjoy a view. The dead will not appreciate the scenery, nor will they hear the music or benefit from the air conditioning.

An inexpensive gravesite may well save the dollars that will pay college tuition at a later date for the children; and should space be offered in the family plot, the widow should by all means consider it, especially if there would be room for her body should she not remarry.

Despite the high cost of funerals, one must view the funeral director in somewhat of a sympathetic light. He has developed his business around the emotional needs of people who are, for the most part, without the hope of Christ. He himself most often has no hope, and so there is no way for him to know when needs are different because of spiritual resources. Were there no need for expensive funerals, they would not be so readily available; but because death is such a fearful subject to those who face a Christless eternity, they will console themselves with empty ritual and earthly trappings that are useless for eternity.

Funeral directors are trained to help, whatever their spiritual persuasion, and some of their help is aimed at procuring financial assistance for the widow. Marsha's husband had served in the military only a short time before obtaining a medical discharge. Convinced that he did not qualify for any benefits, she only reluctantly allowed the funeral director to make application for Veterans Administration benefits toward burial costs. It was a pleasant surprise to receive their check toward funeral expenses. The Social Security Administration also provides a small lump-sum benefit toward the funeral, but the widow must apply for these benefits herself and in person.

The funeral director is also aware of such details as the number of copies of the death certificate necessary. He takes care of the notification to the local newspaper, ordering of flowers, and even making sure that memorial gifts and flower tags arrive in the widow's hands for proper disposition and acknowledgment. Sympathetic, yet emotionally uninvolved, he is able to consider details that might well be forgotten otherwise.

The notification printed in the newspaper serves several purposes. Obviously, it informs acquaintances within the range of the newspaper's circulation that a person has died and informs them of funeral details. Close friends should be called, and often one of them will offer to call others so that the burden may be lifted from the widow. The obituary columns are also read by banks and lawyers, and it is on this basis that joint checking accounts and savings accounts are frozen until a court order can be obtained to allow the widow to have access to the funds. We shall discuss the implications of this in a later chapter. If a will was made, the lawyer who drew that will is often notified through such a column that it should now be brought to light.

UNFORTUNATELY, the newspaper notification is a signal to some rather unsavory characters, also. Sometimes warped minds use the identification given as opportunity for obscene phone calls. Occasionally thieves use the information concerning funeral time as a license to relieve the widow of her earthly inheritance when they are certain the house will be empty. Tombstone salesmen start calling, often before the casket has been lowered into the ground. Charities of honorable and not-so-honorable intentions are quick to place their bid for donations from the widow's inheritance. Swindlers of every size, type, and description lay the groundwork for their work of deceit.

Such information sounds menacing, but a minimum number of precautions will prevent such events from taking place, and fear should not keep the widow from making the information public.

The menace of obscene phone calls can be eliminated to some degree by leaving the address out of the notice. Provided with a name, however, some callers are difficult to discourage. If this happens, simply ignore what the person is saying and quietly hang up the phone. If the call is repeated, pressing the receiver button and stating something like, "Officer, this is the caller," often scares even the most determined pest away. If the caller persists, do not hesitate to contact the telephone company. They have had much experience with obscene and annoying calls, and are eager to offer their assistance in stopping such offenders from invading your privacy.

A man's relatives and close friends will be at his funeral, and thieves are aware of that fact. Their sympathy does not extend to respecting the feelings of the widow, and they are anxious to invade the empty home. Asking a neighbor to watch the home while it is empty is a wise policy. There are those who secretly dread funerals, and if given an excuse to avoid attending, they will gladly accept it and perform such a service.

Tombstone salesmen are among the many who attempt to capitalize on the emotional upheaval of new widows. The stone will be larger and more expensive if purchased close to the time of death. Contrary to the sales pitch, this "memorial of love" can well wait awhile to be purchased. It cannot be placed, at any rate, until the ground has settled. Unless the grave is on a family plot with matching stones, there is little reason for anything more than a simple metal marker. Monuments to the dead serve little purpose except in the minds of the living, and the purchase price might well make the difference between keeping the car or walking, because the insurance couldn't be afforded. Some cemeteries have done widows a big favor by insisting that all markers be at ground level.

CHARITIES are quick to recognize the fact that widows often inherit money. The legacy of $50,000 may seem a tremendous amount of money at first, and to give some of it away to a worthy cause seems to be of small consequence. As one views the total picture, however, the realization should come that the interest on such an amount is only slightly more than $5,000 per year at even the most excellent rates (as of writing). That is approximately $400 per month, which means that most widows will either have to use the principal to supplement their income or find outside employment. The outlook for total security is not particularly bright in either case. Even if the amount of insurance is as much as $100,000, the widow with children will not live luxuriously and plan for their education at the same time.

If all charities were honest, the problems connected with donations would still be difficult. To decide who is worthy of what is not easy. Also, people who are normally kind, considerate, and well-mannered become quite belligerent when they are soliciting donations for wide-eyed, hungry orphans. When the recipient of the donation is the solicitor himself, the persuasion becomes almost irresistible. The fraudulent campaign may be for a nonexistent institution, or one that is neither aware of nor receiving funds from the solicitor, or one which receives so little of the collected funds that even a sizeable donation is of little effect except the support of the collectors. Whatever the gimmick, the result is wasted money.

The solution to the charities problem is also quite simple. Offer to take the name and address of the organization, and inform the caller that when you are ready to decide the amounts to be given that they will be considered. Any pressure for immediacy of need should alert you to the possibility of fraud. If the need is real, and the organization is carrying on legitimate work, then the donation will still be effective when rational decisions can be made.

Before making any donations, check with the Better Business Bureau in your city. Not only do they publish information concerning frauds to be aware of, but they also provide lists of genuine charities and the percentages which are actually channeled into the work. The small amount of time spent checking the validity and worth of the charities under consideration may mean the difference between real help for those in need and wasted dollars.

The Better Business Bureau also has some interesting information concerning other ruses used to relieve the widow of her money. C.O.D. packages arrive at her door; plastic-encased obituary notices arrive in the mail with the invoices enclosed; expensive Bibles arrive with the widow's name stamped in gold; workmen arrive indicating that they have been hired to pave the driveway or reroof the house; and nurserymen arrive to plant expensive shrubbery.

You are responsible for nothing for which a signed sales order cannot be produced. Unless the company and the order are familiar, C.O.D. packages should not be accepted. Instead of wondering, "Whatever made Charlie do a sweet thing like ordering that Bible for me?" refuse it. He probably didn't order it; it is probably drastically overpriced; and to accept delivery only encourages perpetration of the fraud on others. If Charlie really did order the Bible for you, there will most likely be a signed purchase order that can be produced.

You are not legally bound to pay for any unordered merchandise sent through the mail. Should you receive any such items, you are free to do with them as you please, and after a reasonable length of time you may discard them. Do not yield to any demands for payment; and if such demands become insistent, you may drop a note to the party concerned, informing them that they are free to retrieve their merchandise at any time, after they have reimbursed you for storage charges. The silence following this is usually immediate and profound.

OTHER than the necessary arrangements for the funeral itself, the best advice a woman can heed is DON'T. Don't make any decisions or promises that can possibly be postponed to a later date. Don't pay for unordered merchandise. Don't allow any "previously ordered" work to proceed without signed purchase orders. Even then, most legitimate companies are willing to allow you time to gather your senses about you before proceeding with the work.

Finances are not the only area of caution during this sensitive time. Not only are the emotions of the widow especially vulnerable, but so are those of almost every relative, and many friends and neighbors. Under the pressure of grief many things are said and done which are totally apart from a person's normal pattern of behavior. Aunt Irene's giggling at the funeral home is most likely a nervous reaction to death. Al probably didn't show up because he can't bear to fall apart emotionally in front of others. Mike and Sue talked about the antics of their great-aunt Gussie because they were trying to block out thoughts about the death that were really bothering them. Your best friend avoided you because she couldn't think of anything to say that was meaningful.

Real or imagined slights on the part of relatives and friends should be totally ignored. If it is true that "By this shall all men know that ye are my disciples, if ye have love one to another," then our love will be manifested in forgiving and forgetting what has happened under stress. Widowhood carries with it too many adjustments to add to it the burdens of anger and resentment.

Onc Penny,
Two Pennies

CHAPTER FOUR

One Penny,
Two Pennies

The funeral is over. The furor and the food have diminished, and the only reminders are a crumpled napkin on the floor beside a chair where somebody didn't see it to pick it up, and a plate of leftover ham in the refrigerator. The house is quiet for the first time in three days, and the only reason you don't get up to turn the lights on is because you're too tired to care. You don't even feel like crying; you just want to sleep, and yet the bed is an empty memory that you don't want to face just now. Death has become reality. You are a widow.

Morning brings with it some additional realities; and as the widow proceeds to obtain ready cash to meet her immediate needs, she is brought directly into contact with one of those realities—she cannot even write a check for next week's groceries because the joint checking account has been frozen! The legalities of death must be attended to promptly in order that she might meet day-to-day expenses. The lawyer must be contacted so he can begin to work toward closing the estate; papers must be collected and evaluated; and even though your husband talked about writing a will, you're not sure whether he ever did so. Insurance companies must be contacted, and a source of reliable income must be located in addition to locating funds for immediate use.

WITH all due respect to those brave souls who fought and won the battles that enabled an individual to handle the details involved in settlement of an estate (known as probate), the person who has the time, energy, boldness, and intelligence to carry the procedure through from beginning to end without legal assistance is a rare creature indeed. The paperwork is complicated, court appearances are necessary, and a mistake in any one of a number of details could cause annoying and frustrating delays. For the less than exceptional woman who has anything more than a very simple estate, a lawyer is recommended. Even the initial procedure of obtaining the order for the release of funds in jointly held accounts is made infinitely easier when a lawyer, who knows what to do, can handle the matter.

Handling special accounts, preparing inventories, arranging appraisals, gathering and sorting through financial records, and disposing of personal belongings are difficult enough even when there is a knowledgeable person to explain procedure and warn against dangers. Lawyers are also effective buffers between the widow and those who would attempt to coerce her into unwise decisions. In addition, should some of the details involved in the settlement of the estate go awry, the widow has recourse to her attorney.

Martha's husband leased an expensive, large, late-model

automobile for business purposes. Although the lease was held in the name of the corporation owned by her husband, the lessor tried to insist that Martha assume responsibility for the vehicle. The monthly payments would have exceeded the amount of her social security check, and although there were other funds available, she felt that her budget would not allow for such expenditure. When the lessor became belligerent and threatened to sue the estate, Martha simply called her lawyer and asked him to handle the matter. Within the hour the car was no longer in her possession, and there were never any additional claims pressed.

Louise considered herself fortunate to have her husband's estate settled just a year after his death. The sale of the house because of a move to another state complicated tax settlements for another year, but the overall process was accomplished with relative ease, considering that her husband was self-employed and had died without leaving a will. More than a year later, she received a notice that the state in which the death had occurred was demanding additional taxes on the dissolved business. Pouring over the papers seemed futile; they were complicated and, without a complete review of the entire process from beginning to end, the claim could not be proved one way or the other. The circumstances of her busy life did not allow for the expenditure of time on such an activity. Fortunately, the estate had been handled by a lawyer who had in his files all of the necessary information. The mistake was one which had occurred because of lack of communication between lawyer and accountant, and probably would have been made by any person preparing the papers. The additional taxes had to be paid, but an enormous amount of time and effort had been spared for Louise.

IF THE family has used a lawyer before the husband's death and the widow has confidence in him, a brief visit to his office will set in motion the machinery that will clear the way for settlement of the estate. Generally, he will know if there is a will, and will be familiar with the details of it. He may well have handled legal matters for the family that would have a bearing on the estate.

If there is no lawyer, and none can be recommended by other family members, you may call the local bar association and explain the situation to them. They will gladly supply the names of several reputable men who are capable of handling your affairs. If you prefer a more personal touch, you might ask a businessman you know and trust if he is able to recommend someone he has used.

No matter who recommends the lawyer you turn to, if there is any hint of dishonesty, depart with all haste and seek another lawyer! Aside from the fact that as a Christian you want to set forth a reputation that is completely above board, the lawyer who is willing to be dishonest *for* you is also willing to be dishonest *with* you.

Ruth's husband had entered into a "handshake" agreement several days before his death for the sale of his rowboat and motor. Shortly after the funeral the buyer approached her regarding completion of the sale, and when Ruth checked with her lawyer to determine the legality of disposing of the boat immediately, he advised her to have the man predate the check. She refused to take such action, but continued with the lawyer. Much later, when the court date had been set for the closing of the estate, the lawyer informed her that he had "made a mistake" in computing the charges for the work he had done and had charged her $100 more than he had led her to believe it would cost her. The only way to change the amount was to reschedule the court date, which would involve a delay of several months. He agreed to reimburse her privately if she would not contest the amount at her court appearance. Needless to say, she never saw the $100 in question.

AMONG the documents that must be located for the settlement of estates are insurance policies, bankbooks, wills, any notes that are either payable or receivable, certificates of deposit, copies of recent income tax returns, business agreements, social security number, military discharge papers, claim number for Veteran's Administration, marriage certificate, birth certificate, real estate deeds, and automobile registration. A safe rule to follow is: Don't throw away any document that looks even vaguely official. Insurance policies that appear to have lapsed may simply be "paid up," and stock certificates that have been the family joke for years may be worth cold, hard cash. Even nonofficial-looking documents like a hastily scrawled I.O.U. may be collectible.

It is best to have witnesses present when safety deposit boxes are opened. Such precautions may well quench the fires of angry accusation later if there are those who feel that they have been treated unfairly in a will. Other places to look for papers are strong boxes, desk drawers, personal files, lockers, safes, and briefcases.

As soon as possible, the widow should make application for social security benefits. Although few widows are able to live entirely on the funds received from this source, it is valuable and regular income around which financial planning can be made. A chart showing approximate amounts that a widow can expect to receive is included at the end of this chapter.

To receive social security benefits, one must prove eligibility. If the necessary documents can be presented when you arrive at the social security office, much valuable time and effort can be saved.

1. A certified copy of the death certificate.
2. The social security number of your husband.
3. An estimate of your husband's earnings for the year in which he died, and a record of the earnings for the the previous year should provide the necessary information.
4. A copy of your marriage certificate.
5. Your social security number and the social security

numbers of your children. If they do not have numbers, the social security office will assign them.

6. Birth certificates for yourself and your children. If these records are not available, the social security office will sometimes accept other indications of the date of birth.

If you do not have all of the necessary documents, make application anyway. Social security employees are trained to help, not hinder; and they may be able to assist you in obtaining alternate acceptable proofs.

The widow may be entitled to Civil Service benefits. If her husband was employed in civilian service for the federal government, the widow would do well to determine her eligibility. Such information may be obtained by contacting any federal agency. State and local governments also offer programs for their employees; and if the deceased was employed through one of them, the widow should contact the concerned agencies to determine if there are any benefits due.

Insurance companies should also be notified immediately, including workmen's compensation, should it apply. Many women are not aware that there are various settlement options for insurance policies, and so meekly accept checks for the entire amount of the policies held. The amount, larger than most have ever seen before, appears sufficient for large donations to charity, a new car, and even a short vacation to "get away from it all." Too late, many a woman wakes up to realize that social security funds just won't do for shelter, clothing, and food each month, and with insurance funds gone or seriously depleted, the only alternative is to find a job.

Most companies allow the widow some time to make a decision, and while the options vary from company to company, they are basically quite similar. In the interim, the widow is allowed to withdraw a stated amount immediately and decide on the disposition of the rest of the money later. The company will pay interest on the amount they are holding for her.

When enough time has lapsed so that the widow has had opportunity to realistically appraise her financial situation, she may decide to draw the interest only from the insurance funds, with the right of unlimited withdrawal of the principal at any time. She may opt to draw a life income, with specified amounts to be paid on certain dates for her lifetime. She may also choose to receive the benefits of the insurance policies in agreed amounts over a certain period of time, thus benefiting from both the interest and principal to some degree; or she may decide to leave the entire amount with the insurance company to accumulate interest for security in her own retirement.

A widow who at age thirty-five is the beneficiary of a $15,000 life-insurance policy may receive about $90 per month as guaranteed lifetime income. If she should decide she needs $150 or $200 to supplement her other income, the insurance company will pay her that amount until the funds expire. Such a decision carries with it the risk that her own retirement years will lack sufficient funds for her support, however. She may also elect to receive the $15,000 in a lump-sum payment.

The decision as to how to best utilize insurance funds is one that must be made carefully and in the light of the total economic situation of the family involved. Should an insurance company attempt to railroad a decision, it might be well to contact the lawyer to determine if the company is acting within its rights under the terms of the policy.

WITH some families, the long-term financial situation is no great problem. Careful planning has assured that between social security benefits and insurance payments the widow will lead at least a comfortable, if not a luxurious, life. Unfortunately, all of these benefits take time to become effective, and even for those who planned their paychecks carefully, there is often quite a gap between the end of the last paycheck and the beginning of the first benefit check.

This is not a time to suffer in silence. A month is a long time for anyone to live on oatmeal, and it is for causes like this that churches take special collections. The pastor who does not inquire after the widow's material welfare is rare indeed, and to make the need known is often to have it supplied. Sometimes, generous employers provide an extra month's salary, but this would be the exception rather than the rule. It might not be foolish, however, to call the employer and inquire if perhaps there were additional funds due. Should this resource fail, and the church is unable to help, there may be enough collateral within the estate itself to enable borrowing from the bank on a short-term basis. A paid-for car, snowmobile, or boat may well have enough worth so that the bank will loan the widow sufficient money to carry on until other funds become available. Although she still retains the use of the item, she will not be able to sell it until the money has been repaid to the bank. If none of those avenues are open, social services and welfare agencies are available for help in times of emergency.

AS THE widow gathers together the financial obligations of the family, she should determine whether or not any of the bills due had an automatic paid-up provision. Installment loans such as those for automobiles, sporting equipment, and sometimes even homes often have this insurance attached to them, as do some credit cards. Each company should be contacted to determine if such a provision existed. It will be her responsibility to pay the bills still due, and the lawyer will advise about the special account necessary to accomplish this end.

It takes time to settle an estate, and that time varies greatly depending upon whether or not there was a will, how quickly all of the beneficiaries can be located, and the settlement of business details. A widow cannot wait until the estate is settled to decide her standard of living. As soon as she is fairly certain of the amount of income she will have, it is time to evaluate her expenses in relation to them.

An automobile is more than just a weekly stop to fill the gas tank. Any payments that might still be due, license fees, and insurance must also be considered. If the car is an older model, she must determine whether or not the repairs required will be a financial burden. She will have to decide if the car is really a necessary expense or just an expensive luxury.

Mary's husband had driven a large, expensive automobile in his business, and often enjoyed "puttering around" with Mary's older, smaller car. She felt that neither vehicle met her needs as the larger, newer car consumed large amounts of gas and was difficult to park. The smaller vehicle she had used not only needed tires, but gave trouble starting and made noises that even her untrained ear discerned as less than normal operation. The solution was to sell both automobiles and purchase a new, small car which was easy for her to handle, inexpensive to operate, and gave trouble-free operation.

A home, too, is more than just the surface expense of monthly payments. Often, after widowhood, payments are no longer a problem as the insurance has taken care of the principal due. The age of the home must be considered. Will the upkeep be a financial strain? What about the furnace? The water heater? The roof? Beside the financial expense, what about the physical upkeep? The lawn will have to be mowed, the trim will probably need painting on a regular basis (as minimum maintenance), and the inside will need paint and repair from time to time. What about the neighborhood? Is it a place where it is safe for a woman to live alone? Are there neighbors who will be able and willing to offer assistance when it is needed?

Weighed against an apartment, a home might well be worth the extra effort and expense to keep. Purchased at $25,000 at an interest rate of 6 percent, it may well sell for $40,000. However, it will cost $40,000, and possibly more, to replace, and that at a rate of 9 percent or better. At that rate, only a few hundred dollars of the principal is paid off in the first year! An apartment offers no equity; there is no accumulation of worth to be used as security in later years. Also, the same apartment that is worth $100 or $150 per month now will most probably double in cost within ten years. This is a rate of inflation that cannot be borne on a fixed income. However, it may be such a drain to keep a home that ultimate security is being sacrificed to do so.

Marge's home was a large old farmhouse which had been in the family for several generations. She considered selling only the land which surrounded the site, but soon was faced with expensive roof repairs, expensive heating bills, and the need to either paint the house or reside it with aluminum. The funds required were far in excess of what she thought she could reasonably spend. She found instead a smaller house located in a residential area of a nearby city which would be paid for entirely by the sale of the house and land on which she lived. Not only did it offer financial security, but the nearness of neighbors provided a sense of ready help if she should ever need it.

Insurance must also be reviewed. Term insurance will provide money for the education of the children if the widow should die before it expires, but if she lives there is no benefit for either her or her children. The premiums are higher on a policy which would have retirement value for the widow, but she may well appreciate that decision when the time has passed for her to be employed. Life insurance for children is a kind thought, especially if that insurance guarantees their right to purchase insurance later in life. To the woman who is trying to make ends meet, however, minimal policies would be a wiser decision.

When all expenses and all sources of income have been weighed against each other, the widow is ready to consider whether or not she will have to be employed. If she has no children, the decision may well hinge upon having something to do. If she has children, the consideration must be for their welfare. The children who have a widowed mother are just as much, if not more, in need of her attention and talents as they were while their father was alive.

After a given amount, the widow's social security benefits

are reduced one dollar for every two dollars she earns. Unless she earns a sufficient amount to totally supplement her children's benefits, it may be that she is losing a great deal by opting for employment. Perhaps she could make up the deficiency of income from social security by practicing economy of living rather than working at an outside job. Learning to sew or learning to shop more economically might make a great amount of difference in the family budget.

If the necessity of working cannot be avoided, then the widow must decide whether to revive old skills or to learn new ones. "Brush-up" courses impress employers, and they often are willing to hire women at higher levels of pay than those who have not had such training. If a woman has no skills, or would rather not return to the type of job she had before, she might be able to delay employment long enough to learn new skills. Secretarial courses, key-punch courses, and accounting courses have all opened new vistas to women who would otherwise have been destined to serve hamburgers for the rest of their lives.

WHILE the widow is dealing with a lawyer for the settlement of the estate, there is one more important step she should take. She should prepare or update her will. We state it now, and it cannot be repeated too often, *it is more important for a widow to have a will than it is for a married couple!* The widow can better determine who would be the best guardians of her children spiritually, psychologically, and financially than any court-appointed guardian. If she does not make the decision, others may have to.

A lawyer is the only one who can properly prepare a will. The law does not recognize good intentions, nor does it heed hastily scribbled deathbed notes. The best practice is to make an appointment and then do it.

Self-prepared wills are a hazard. Even carefully prepared documents are liable to errors which may make an entire will null and void, or distribute proceeds in a way which is entirely contrary to intentions. Legal language is precise, and only those especially trained are qualified to know the effects of such language.

A will prepared by a lawyer is an available will. As we stated before, one of the purposes of printing the death notice in the paper is so that those who are in possession of wills may be notified.

A lawyer is also able to warn against certain conditions and restrictions. While it may seem good to you to give your money to a dear niece only if she attends a certain Bible college, that institution may not be able to meet her needs when the time for her to go to college arrives, or it may have altered its position so radically on some important doctrine that it would be unwise for her to attend. The limitations of the will could seriously injure her opportunities for precisely the kind of education you intended for her to have.

Finally, having just been through the difficult and expensive funeral procedure, you are in a position to determine what your funeral will be like. You can specify an inexpensive casket and a simple ceremony and relieve your loved ones of that decision and expense. What blessed hope we have, knowing that if we are "absent from the body" we are "present with the Lord" (2 Cor. 5:8). Relieved of the need to exalt our remains, we can leave a testimony that few will be able to ignore.

Examples of Monthly Social Security Payments (effective June 1976)[1]

Average Yearly Earnings of Husband After 1950*

Benefits can be paid to a:	$923 or less	$3,000	$4,000	$5,000	$6,000	$8,000	$10,000
Disabled worker	107.90	223.20	262.20	304.50	344.10	427.80	474.00
Wife under 65 and one child in her care	54.00	118.00	186.20	257.40	287.20	321.00	355.60
Widow or widower caring for one child	162.00	334.80	394.00	456.80	516.20	641.80	711.00
Widow or widower caring for two children	162.00	341.20	448.80	561.90	631.30	748.70	829.50
Child of disabled worker	54.00	111.60	131.30	152.30	172.10	213.20	237.00
Child of deceased worker	107.90	167.40	197.00	228.40	258.10	320.90	355.50
Maximum family payment	161.90	341.20	443.80	561.90	631.30	748.70	829.50

*Generally, average earnings are figured over the period from 1951 until the worker reaches retirement age, becomes disabled, or dies. Up to 5 years of low earnings or no earnings can be excluded. The maximum earnings creditable for social security are $3,600 for 1951-1954; $4,200 for 1955-1958; $4,800 for 1959-1965; $6,600 for 1966-1967; $7,800 for 1968-1971; $9,000 for 1972; $10,800 for 1973; $13,200 for 1974; $14,100 for 1975; and $15,300 for 1976. But average earnings cannot reach these latter amounts until later. Because of this, the benefits shown in the last 2 columns on the right generally will not be payable until future years.

[1] U. S. Department of Health, Education, and Welfare, Social Security Administration, HEW Publication No. (SSA) 76-10033, June, 1976.

Security Is . . .

CHAPTER FIVE

Security Is . . .

Children react somewhat differently to grief; and in our eyes, some seem not to grieve at all. Allan asked every likeable man at the funeral to be his new father; a young girl declared bluntly that she hated God, "because He is so mean"; and another youngster almost destroyed himself with guilt because of the conviction that his father's fatal accident was his fault. For many, the loss of a parent is their first encounter with death, and they are not aware of all the implications that such an event has in their lives. There is simply no experience to tell them how to react to such a loss, and apparent misbehavior is not uncommon.

A child's confusion might well be paralleled to a visit to a

65

church of another denomination, one with a liturgical service. One is fully aware that a response is expected, but the nature of that response remains a mystery until the moment of performance. Sooner or later one finds oneself standing when he should be sitting or kneeling when he should be standing. One mistake leads to embarrassment, and then to another mistake, and only as a reliable example is found is the situation redeemable. A woman's reaction to the death of her husband will be mirrored in her children, and probably determine to a great extent their lifelong reaction to death. Self-pity on their mother's part only confuses and frustrates children. If they see their mother yielding to tears at every minor frustration, no doubt they will soon choose the same avenue of escape from their problems. The natural tendency of children to recover from the loss within a short period of weeks, or months at most, is thwarted. Instead of building toward new lives, they are scarred by the loss of the old. Rather than learning to solve problems on their own, they yield to self-pity and defeat.

A COMMON response to death is the "great American tradition" of eulogy. Unfortunately, this tribute to the dead is often at the expense of the living. Children need a realistic sense of identity with their father, but the man who is presented as the epitome of pure virtue does little to help children adjust to the realities of life. A child may well reason that if her father was so very good, then "God must be mean" to have taken him away. Not by any means do we wish to encourage the idea that death is God's sure punishment for a man's sins; but we must at the same time understand the workings of a child's mind and work to show that God always acts in a loving and kind manner.

If the mother should remarry, the effects of eulogizing a father can be disastrous in a second way. The man the mother marries will be a fallible human being who can never hope to live up to the standards of perfection that have been set before him ("Daddy *never* lost his temper"). The same sort of trap exists for the mother. Believing all she has said about her "perfected" previous husband, the adjustments to living with an imperfect man under real-life conditions are sometimes beyond the realm of human achievement.

A third effect of the eulogy tradition becomes apparent only as the children mature and seek mates of their own. Their father has been the ideal, the perfect image. The marriage their parents had was, according to all reports, without fault or argument; and this is the standard they have set for themselves. They will never be able to meet this standard, and by our maintenance of the myth we have jeopardized their chance at happiness.

SELF-PITY is not limited to widows. Children, too, love to dump all of their problems into the barrel marked "Dad died." The broken bicycle, the dreary afternoon, the fight at school would all be different, ". . . if dad were still here." Sometimes simple understanding and a quiet discussion of the ways God uses to teach us the lessons we need to know or a simple diversion like a shopping trip or a spontaneous picnic are all that are needed to turn the course of the day. Sometimes, the blunt realization that ". . . if dad were still here" things wouldn't be any different than they are right now places the blame precisely on target. Eleven-year-old Steve tearfully blamed a depressing day on the fact that he missed his father. The only problem with this appraisal was that his father had died some three years earlier. An honest evaluation of the situation revealed that his play for sympathy revolved around the fact that he didn't want to clean his room. It is highly probable that many of the "problems" that arise will be found to have a similar basis.

Some social situations do come up that cause honest feelings of "being left out." These are not impossible situations, and children can be helped through them. Just two days after Joan's husband died, her son's school sponsored their annual "Fathers' Breakfast." Feeling that it was more important for her seven-year-old son to be in school than to sit at home feeling sorry for himself, she contacted the school principal and alerted him to the situation so that the boy would be under watchful eyes throughout the day. A kindly neighbor who had a son in the same grade as Joan's boy volunteered to be a substitute father for the morning. The following year, the church choir director volunteered for the substitute position. Not only did these men help her son over two otherwise difficult days, but it also gave him the privilege of having a "father" at the breakfast. Business obligations had in the past kept his own father away! Likewise, "father/son" banquets can be easily substituted by uncles, grandfathers, or family friends, and there is little need for children to miss these events. If for some reason a substitute cannot be found, the effects need not be traumatic. Two or three missed events in the course of a year may be disappointing, but children are usually agreeable to substitution. If it is impossible to replace the event with another activity, often a toy or an addition to a favorite hobby will more than suffice without the implication of "buying" the child.

JUST as self-pity is not confined to widows, neither is guilt. Children come up with some surprisingly convincing reasons for blaming themselves for their father's death. Often that feeling of guilt is not expressed except in rebellion or a withdrawn attitude. Sometimes it finds no expression at all until much later, except in the broken heart of the child who bears it. The causes for such feelings range from misbehavior on the child's part to the transmission of a contagious disease, from evil thoughts to feelings of personal inadequacy. One young boy spent many years blaming himself for his father's death in an automobile accident, which happened when the child was only seven years old. The day before the fatality he had been "washing the car" for his father with a squirt gun and had squirted some water on the hub caps. He firmly believed that the water had gotten into the brakes and caused them to fail, thus causing his father's accident. No matter how far-fetched the story sounds to our ears, to him it was true, and his guilt feelings were just as real as if he had actually caused the brakes to fail.

So often we omit the details when we talk to children about death, and those details are the very ones that could free them from guilt. It's not morbid to talk about what causes heart attacks or why cars have accidents. It may give a whole new direction to a child's life to know that God doesn't take parents away because of bad thoughts or misbehavior or an unappreciative attitude.

BESIDES being emotional beings, children are physical beings, and very practical ones at that. It doesn't take long for them to realize that it was daddy who went to work each day and brought home a paycheck to meet the family needs. Obviously, money is going to have to come from somewhere. Few are as brash in seeking to meet the need as six-year-old Allan who went about on the day of the funeral asking various men he liked if they would be his new daddy now; but most children are aware that the need must be met from somewhere. Allan finally expressed himself in more concrete terms when he looked at his mother with some degree of concern about three days after the funeral and asked, "When are you going to go to work?" His relief was immense when informed that such a step would not be necessary for the present because the government would be sending them some money every month to buy food and clothes and the bicycle tire necessary to replace the one that had gone flat.

A detailed explanation of financial matters is not necessary, but assurance that needs will be adequately met can relieve young minds of burdens they need not bear. If it should be necessary for a mother to work, most children are not resentful if an adequate explanation is given concerning the reasons for the necessity and the arrangements for their care.

Children are also clever. Even those who cannot add are able to deduce that if one parent has died, the chances of losing both parents have just increased by 100 percent. Mother often comes to the same conclusion at about the same time and half-heartedly thinks of someone who might be willing to take her children in the event of her death. Children's questions are often answered in a casual-sounding way with, "You don't have to worry about that," or "Oh, probably Aunt Mary or Grandma Jones." The subject is then dropped and never again resurrected. If mom should die, the discussions and arguments over who should take the children, or who should take which of the children are loud and bitter, often resulting in reshuffling and inadequate care. *It is more important for a widow to have a valid, current will than it is for a married couple.* The chances of both marriage partners dying at the same time are slim. If a widow should die, there is often no person who is capable of making the correct decisions as to the distribution of the children. In addition to the family divisions caused over such matters, the degradation to the child's self-esteem may well be irreparable. Imagine being the center of an argument over who is going to take "Millie's kid"—with the knowledge that none of the parties really wants the responsibility.

Before you make a will, be sure to ask the parties you want to take your children if they would be willing to accept the responsibility! It seems banal to state such an obvious fact, but one pastor's wife reports that if all the parents who had willed their children to them without their knowledge had died, they would have been the legal guardians of more than twenty children! Imagine the surprise of waking up some morning with twenty (or even three) cherub-faced children on your doorstep, for whom you were expected to provide food, clothing, and education until they reached the age of eighteen, whose parents you hadn't even seen for several years.

In addition to asking the prospective parents of your children, it might also be helpful to ask your children whom they might choose to live with. Lois's choice of a young couple to care for her son in case of her death seemed ideal, until her son pointed out to her that he would be out of place in that family of girls some four years younger than he. His personal choice was a more mature couple who already had two boys in their family with whom he shared friendship. Religious background, attitudes, and mutual agreement produced a situation that was, in the long run, much more secure.

Depending on the relationship of the substitute parents and the children in question, information should be provided which would benefit them. A widow may be aware that her child is allergic to penicillin, but the child may not know it, and the first illness in the new home could have tragic results. One shy young lady of about eight was terrified of cats. Too bashful to tell her guardians about the problem, she lay awake in terror for several nights while the family cat roamed freely throughout the house. Her problem was discovered one night when the cat jumped on her bed and she screamed; but many nights of discomfort could have been avoided if the information had been previously supplied. Such information should be updated from time to time for accuracy's sake, and the child's participation in providing the information would not only make it more relevant, but certainly would add to his sense of security.

Changes are upsetting to children, and the more gradually they can be made, the more willingly they will be accepted. One change that should be guarded against with all diligence is that of an altered relationship with paternal grandparents. Sometimes this is a relationship that is difficult to maintain because of attitudes or distance. Part of security is belonging, and part of the heritage of our children is with their father's parents. It is often well worth personal discomfort and expense to continue seeing these people on a regular basis. At minimum, an effort should be made to maintain correspondence, even if we must constantly supply the encouragement.

Coping with the financial problems of widowhood sometimes results in radically altered standards of living. It takes

71

time to evaluate just what changes must be made and what can be managed with careful budgeting; and it is well worthwhile from the children's point of view if help can be accepted from family, church, and/or social organizations to forestall these changes, with the result that some of them may not be necessary.

Sometimes security comes in furry packages. Loneliness often needs to hold something that is warm and live and belongs to just him. The beauty of such a solution is that warm, furry, live things like to be held for very limited periods of time before they want to play. That is just the action that will scatter self-pity to the wind. "Clifford," who grew from five pounds to ninety-five pounds in the space of a year, may have been more dog than most families are willing to cope with, but his antics and loving nature were a perfect solution for the only child for whom he was purchased. The sound of laughter was rich reward for the small price of housebreaking. Smaller dogs, cats, and kittens are, likewise, most valuable "therapy" for children at a time like this.

NO MATTER how the widow manages, someone will always be available to tell her what she's doing wrong. She's either too strict, insisting that her children help with household chores, or too permissive, allowing them to ride to the grocery store three blocks away to purchase a well-earned treat. She either holds them too close by demanding that they be in before dark or pays them too little attention when she hires a babysitter so she can have an evening out. She dresses her children too extravagantly when she purchases new winter jackets at the January sales or too shabbily when she sends them out to play in their old torn jackets in March (never mind that everyone else is wearing old torn jackets in March—the widow's children are the ones who get noticed). It is in the area of discipline that the widow gains sure knowledge of why God planned for two parents in each family—they need to reinforce each other against the critics. In the areas the neighbors don't criticize, the children themselves will find ways to shake her confidence.

Self-control is essential, as is self-knowledge. A widow can't afford a nebulous concept of what she thinks discipline should be. Knowledge of her children's needs and the factors which constitute good discipline are essential if the family situation is to remain in control and produce children who are capable of responsible, productive adult lives.

Just as children share in adult problems of guilt and self-pity, so adults share the childhood problem of the "Dad died" barrel. "If only Mike were alive . . ." is the plaintive cry of many a widow. It's the easy thing to do. More realistically, the problems may be caused by a lack of present discipline, the lack of organization, the lack of spiritual guidance, or any one of a number of things correctable by the widow's hand. Torn jackets, dirty ears, and uncombed hair are easily corrected problems. Disrespectful attitudes and hard-to-manage children may best be handled by reference to one of several excellent books concerning discipline. Sometimes the problems are carry-overs from incorrect two-parent discipline, and the widow had best face the fact that "having Mike back again" wouldn't change the situation much. Professional help from school authorities, church leaders, and community services may be the wise course of action before present problems become unmanageable.

As a rule, children who were well-disciplined in a two-parent home will probably be well-disciplined in a one-parent home. They want to know the boundaries for their behavior no matter how many parents they have, and they will respond to proper discipline no matter how many parents administer it. In addition, God has promised to be Father to the fatherless. This is not an empty promise, and many a widow has seen the visible effects of His intervention in the lives of her children. Joey, age ten, was of a particularly independent nature, and that nature often led to clashes with his mother. She began to turn these situations over to the Father, often with the words, "Lord, You promised to be a Father to him, and he needs a Father right now." Invariably, Joey would come from his room to which he had angrily stomped some moments before and apologize for his defiant action. The angry sessions stopped within a few short months, and peace was restored because of the Father's influence in that home.

Security may be a lot of things, but to a child it is knowing that his needs, both physical and emotional, will be met. A mother who is confident in God's care of her and her children will radiate that confidence to her children. The critics will try to convince the widow that to raise a child without a father is to raise a weak, self-pitying individual who will never lead a productive, happy life. What those critics do not take into consideration is that the fatherless child falls under the special consideration of the heavenly Father, who is not limited by mortal considerations. A child secure in His love is a fortunate child indeed.

How Does Your Garden Grow?

CHAPTER SIX

How Does Your Garden Grow?

The critics, with their smatterings of Freudian psychology, have overlooked some important factors in human adaptability. We have no quarrel with the concept that sex education is more than the facts about the birds and the bees, but argue violently against the idea that Johnny will not mature into a properly functioning adult because he doesn't see mom and dad holding hands every day.

The relationship between parents is important, and if the child was old enough at the time of his father's death to have memories of that relationship, much is gained. Realistic recollections, however, also build images that can serve as models. "Your father knew that I loved gladiolas, and every August he

77

would bring them home to me by the armloads," tells much about loving response. "When your dad and I painted the garage . . ." or "cleaned the basement" or "put in the garden" says more about working together than any abstract statement about responsibility. "He didn't like liver, and I didn't like the lonely feeling when he went hunting, so I always invited a friend in to eat liver during hunting season," demonstrates cooperation and consideration in a way no sermon could ever accomplish.

If all Johnny ever saw, however, was the relationship between his parents, he would be missing out on a vital part of his total education. He needs to see his mother's relationship to all other men—her father, her brothers, her brothers-in-law, family friends, cousins, and neighbors. He needs to know that she acts differently with uncles than she does with neighbors, and that brothers-in-law are different from close friends.

Allan, the little matchmaker at his father's funeral, eventually resumed his quest for a father, but under a different guise. Sensing the need for male influence in the home, he would eagerly suggest to his mother that "the man who works at the filling station would make a nice dad," or "Mom, you should marry Mr. Jones, I like him." These suggestions became perfect opportunities to explain quietly the fact that Allan's choice was already married, or fifteen years too young (or old), or that the man he had chosen was of the wrong religious persuasion or not available because of a variety of other reasons. He was also gently informed that women just don't go around asking men to marry them. Allan didn't stop wanting a dad, but he did learn to take his requests to the proper Authority, and is now waiting with patience for the answer to his prayers. At the same time, he has been made to realize that marriage to the wrong person would be far worse than no marriage at all, and is willing to wait for the Lord's time and choice.

Johnny (or Suzy) is also able to learn much from watching other couples as they relate to each other. He knows that Aunt

Sarah and Uncle Joe don't speak pleasantly to each other, and he knows that he wouldn't like to live in a home such as theirs. He knows that your neighbor is nicer to the lady next door than he is to his own wife, and is uncomfortable with that arrangement. He also sees when Aunt Sally and Uncle Mike smile at each other across the room, and it's usually Uncle Mike's lap that he climbs onto during family gatherings. He sees grandmothers and grandfathers, cousins, friends, and people at church on Sunday, and from the positive and negative examples they provide he is able to see that there are differences among families. Discussing these differences, without going into minute detail, can show him the attitudes that make a family happy or unhappy and provide the grounds on which to build his own future.

A YOUNG boy does *not* become "the man of the house" on the day his father dies. Those thoughtless individuals who suggest such a thing should have a string tied around their tongues for a few days to help them remember to think before they speak. Not only does a young boy fail to grow from childhood to manhood during the course of a funeral, but the responsibility placed on the child by such an implication is far too great for him to bear. It denies the childhood that is essential to his proper development. A boy's natural protective attitude toward his mother will give him enough trouble without the added burden of adult responsibility being thrust upon him.

Nine-year-old David was so concerned for his mother every time she had so much as a head-cold that he would carry his pillow and blanket into her room and sleep on the floor beside her bed, "just to make sure you're okay, mom." His reaction stemmed from natural concern.

Eleven-year-old John felt responsible for everything from taking out the garbage to making sure the family got to church on time. His situation got entirely out of hand when he decided to surprise his mother by painting the front hall. His attitude was fostered by a grandmother who insisted that he become "the man in the family."

Irene's forceful insistence that her son fill the adult male role in the family by imposing upon him an endless stream of chores and restricting his contact with his peers by demanding his companionship on shopping expeditions and personal visits to her friends caused an irreparable rift. Physically, her son was capable of handling all of the tasks assigned to him. Mentally and emotionally he rebelled against the responsibility and eventually against the source of that pressure.

Just as the child does not become mature at the funeral, neither does the widow become both mother and father to her offspring. It is usually the same individual who suggests both heresies, and for such the string should be tied with a double knot. Despite the women's liberation movement, females are just not equipped to be fathers, either physically or emotionally. Few women can pitch a ball like a man, or shoot baskets, or play "horsey-back" with any degree of effectiveness. They may fish and hunt and camp, but cannot provide the "man talk" that goes along with such activities. A woman's point of view is entirely different, for the most part, from a man's. The center of her life is her home and family, even if she is employed outside of the home. The hub of a man's world, however, is often his occupation. Family is important to him, but it is only one aspect of his life.

Masculine influence is important for children. It is just as important for girls as it is for boys, for it is by such relationships that girls learn to relate to the males in their adult lives. Grandfathers, uncles, and older cousins are the ideal solution for teaching those relationships.

Marsha's three glowing, well-adjusted teen-age daughters are prime examples of what a healthy relationship with in-laws can accomplish. Although the father had not been a positive influence in the family, his parents took over with loving concern for the girls. Saturday with Grandma and Grandpa and secret plans to "surprise mom" filled their lives with the knowledge that they were lovingly cared for. All three girls have excellent attitudes toward dating and men, and they look forward to marriage some day.

Where family influence is lacking, others can often supply. This is an ideal ministry through the church, and the widow who hasn't been approached on the subject might do well to suggest it to the pastor. Unmarried young people, both college and career, are sometimes willing to take time out of their schedules for such responsibility when they are shown the value of such a ministry. The young couple who haven't any children of their own might be willing to give the time necessary. Should these two avenues fail, "foster grandparents" might prove an excellent solution. Often older couples live far away from their own grandchildren and have plenty of time in which to shower love and attention on a youngster. Male influence need not be "under fifty" to be valid. Two widows found an ideal solution for male companionship for their sons. Living in a town in which a Christian college was located, they were able to have college students spend time with their children as part of a service program.

Organizations for boys and girls which provide male leadership are excellent, but they cannot provide the individual attention the youngsters need. Ideally, there should be at least one consistent positive male influence in the life of a child.

CHILDREN learn by example, and often that principle is totally ignored when widows must work. The children are "dropped off" at one place or another for reasons which sometimes amount to little more than convenience. If a relative is willing to watch a child at no charge or for a very small price, all further considerations of qualification are disregarded. If a neighbor offers convenience of location as well as economy of service, the question is settled. Although children are able to tell the difference in attitudes and actions, they will be confused when they are required to live by two different standards. Often they will choose the easier path and follow the negative example.

As far as possible, it is wise for the widow to be particular about those who care for her children. To find, as Sally did, that your children are involved with drugs as a result of the lack of proper supervision in the home that cared for them is a sad price to pay for convenience. The neighbor who accepted the responsibility for Sally's children provided little more than a place to watch television when the weather was bad. The two junior high children learned to smoke "pot" at a friend's home some two miles distant from their own, at a time when they were considered "home from school."

THERE is another example we must provide. We may have provided "big brothers" or "substitute fathers" or "foster grandparents" in sufficient numbers to meet the needs of a dozen children. We may have the ideal child-care situation in which a dependable, moral, loving woman shows up at the front door every day for a mere pittance and is content to stay for as long as necessary; but until we have provided the spiritual foundation for our children to build on we have done nothing for them. Genesis 44:34 poses a poignant question which might well be spiritualized in every family. "For how shall I go up to my father, and the lad be not with me?" Until we are sure that our children are eternally safe, our parenthood has been in vain. To send a child into the world without Christ, no matter how polished his manners or how bright his mind, is like launching a leaky boat with a new paint job—it will sink. ——

Again, example is important. A child's concept of what God is like closely corresponds with his concept of the earthly father image. If there is no father, then what about the substitutes provided? Are they reliable? Do they live clean, moral lives? Are they honest? Do they fulfill their responsibility to the children out of love, or are they doing somebody a favor?

Secondly, the widow's own Christian experience is important. Her knowledge of the wise and loving action of God in her life may well be the catalyst that makes the children's faith a living reality. They won't settle for empty words, no matter what their ages. They live too close to be fooled by lip service, and will settle for nothing but the heartfelt expression of pure truth.

Alex, age eleven when his father died, was educated in parochial schools. The sight of his mother participating in church activities was a familiar one to him, but he was totally unimpressed. She spoke loudly of "trusting the Lord," but Alex knew that the expression merely indicated that she didn't know what else to do in any given situation. Tirades of temper at even minor frustrations were evidence that she wasn't trusting anybody. He winced when he heard her speak of "the Lord's will." Their bedroom doors were not so far apart that he couldn't hear her nightly sobs with accusations directed at his father's photograph of desertion and unfairness. Alex rejected both his mother and her faith.

Steve, on the other hand, at age seven witnessed the quiet assurance that God was still in control. Just because the reasons for the apparent tragedy were not evident seemed no cause to be afraid. He missed his dad terribly, but he shared his mother's confidence that all was as it should be. One evening while his mother was away on an errand, he was able to explain the means of salvation to his fifteen-year-old babysitter and prayed with her regarding the matter. When his mother returned home some hours later, the babysitter shared the good news of what had taken place. The prayer of thanksgiving that was offered was a joyous one, indeed. While this is not a typical example by any means, it does demonstrate the possibilities.

Examples of God's care are only examples where proper credit is given. Leslie's Christian neighbors did not contribute to any "fund" at the funeral. Instead, they informed her that they were giving their time to her and her children. They kept that promise, and their presence and understanding helped the family over many rough spots emotionally. Only as God was thanked for bringing those kind people into their lives did the children see the true source of the gift.

Immediately after her husband's death, a fine Christian couple moved next door to Sharon. When it became necessary for her to work, they provided all babysitting—free of charge. Again, the children were inclined to give credit to the neighbors, and only as they saw the true source of the gift were they able to give proper response to the Giver.

Family devotions are as important in the one-parent family as they are when both parents are present. Studying Scripture, discussing practical application, and praying together are the substance from which family unity is made. They are necessities which a family can ill afford to be without. Praying together over family and individual concerns and sharing those answers will knit a family together as little else can.

When Doris and her two daughters saw the salvation of a beloved uncle after holding the need before the Lord for almost six months, their common joy brought them even closer together than they had been before.

When Joy prayed in morning devotions for help through a day into which too many things had been crowded, her children were scarcely prepared for the direct answer they received. Just as their mother was about to prepare dinner that evening, a neighbor came to the door with a steaming bowl of spaghetti, their favorite dish. Not only was family unity advanced that night, but faith in God who answers prayer was established in a way that might otherwise have taken months or years to accomplish.

Family devotions are an excellent method of teaching biblical truth to children. Brief lessons geared to specific age levels are often long-remembered. Bible book studies are enjoyable paths to understanding when the children are old enough. One doesn't need to be a Bible school graduate to understand what the Word of God says, and any one of several study booklets can be helpful to those who feel unsure of themselves. Christian bookstores have many good ones, your pastor might be able to suggest some helpful ones, and often one or two are listed in Christian magazines.

When these home studies are reinforced by regular attendance at a Bible-teaching church, they become the springboards to Christian maturity for those who have participated in them.

PAY attention to your children. Widowhood is often fraught with extra duties. Instead of two to do the work, there is only one. Often, in the rush, we get our priorities mixed up. It may be important to get the lawn mowed, and surely the garage needs cleaning from time to time, and the screens need to be changed, but none of these jobs is as important as the future lives of our children. If your children don't think they are important to you, they certainly won't think they are important to God. If they aren't old enough to work with you on some of the household tasks so that they may be done quickly, get help to do them so you can spend more time molding those lives that have been entrusted to you.

Play with your children. What you play isn't really all that important. What counts is the time you are taking from other things just to be with them, the time you are taking to talk to them and learn more about them, the recognition you are giving them as individuals.

Spend effort on your children. When their father was alive, the nights that daddy wasn't home for dinner often turned into paper plate, macaroni-and-cheese nights. When daddy isn't home at all for dinner, the attitude often carries over on a permanent basis, What was once a diversion, a change of routine, begins to tell the children that they just aren't important enough to fuss over.

Jean countered this attitude with her two young children by declaring "dress-up nights" twice a month. She would prpare the children's favorite dishes (hot dogs one week, spaghetti another), set the table with her finest china, and put on a pretty dress. Company was never invited in on these nights—they were for the children alone. Not only did the children see themselves as special because of the attention paid them, but they acquired a set of table manners and attitudes that served well when eating out or when guests were present.

Declare a family night. Marge and her children reserved Monday evening for themselves. They began by visiting the local "hamburger dispensary," then did some shopping to dispose of allowances received the weekend before. They finished the evening by playing games. The order of events was not important, but what did count with the children was that they knew this evening was theirs.

Children who are well-loved and secure, who have a positive regard for their own worth, are children who can relate well to their heavenly Father. The time and effort we spend to encourage the proper attitudes are time and effort well spent. What parent does not rejoice when children who are well-adjusted and happy and in right relationship to God go out into the world? Many are surprised to find that in the accomplishing of the long-range goals there is another, more immediate benefit as they learn to enjoy their children, and often find that they look forward to the activities as much as the youngsters.

"I Will Never
Leave Thee"

CHAPTER SEVEN

"I Will Never Leave Thee"

One day the wedding ring is removed, at least for the majority of younger widows. Whatever the outward reason, be it for cleaning, or hand cream, or simply to wash the evening dishes, it suddenly seems silly to put it back on again. For awhile the widow is self-conscious of that naked white finger, almost as if she had forgotten some essential item of clothing, and then the marks left by that identifying band fade and disappear. The marks never quite leave her heart, however, and it would be foolish to imagine that a relationship like marriage could be erased from the mind like chalk from a blackboard.

Memories, properly used as reminders of happiness, are

good things to treasure. The paths of least resistance tend toward the extremes of eulogy or despair. "He was the perfect husband. I don't know how I'll live without him," or "He was unfair to leave me so I'm just going to get rid of everything and start over," are both defeating. Neither prepares for living in the here and now.

Some reminders may be too much. Ann lived in the past amid photographs, books, and personal belongings. She cooked the meals her husband had preferred, watched the TV programs he had most favored, and continued to subscribe to his favorite sports magazines. One visitor was so perplexed by her life style and attitudes that he inquired whether her husband had passed away or was merely gone on a business trip.

On the other hand, in an effort to rid themselves of any possible source of hurt, some widows dispose of every earthly reminder of their mate. Personal belongings, clothing, photographs, books, and his favorite chair are given to the first person who will take them from the house, or are hastily donated to a local charity or thrown away. In less emotional days to come, these decisions are often regretted. Laura sold the house, the car, and all of the furniture for prices far below their actual value just to be rid of them. She felt that the sacrifice was worth it just to be rid of painful reminders. She then departed for a lengthy vacation at a southern resort. When sanity returned, she found that not only were all of the mementos of her married life destroyed, but the funds used to finance her leave of absence from reality had seriously depleted her assets. She simply did not have enough money to replace the home, car, and furniture which she now needed. She finally rented a small apartment, but was forced to seek employment in order to maintain a comfortable life standard which was, nonetheless, devoid of emotional or financial security.

Some things cause unnecessary emotional trauma, and should be removed as soon as possible. Clothing is a major example of this, and many widows find that the sooner clothing can be given away, the sooner they find rest. Cathy discovered this one evening when she awakened from an especially vivid dream about her husband. The sense of his presence was so intense that she called out his name. The source of the illusion was not difficult to trace. Having gone to bed extremely tired after a busy day, she had forgotten to close the closet door. The odors that she had subconsciously associated with her husband had clung to his clothes, and the mingling of aftershave, leather, and smoke had made the dream seem to be reality. The closet was emptied the next day.

Every widow must decide for herself, on an individual basis, what memories she can handle. To some, personal jewelry, libraries, or sporting equipment—even those which could be used by family members—cause too much pain to be worth keeping. To others, there is very little that will upset them. Marcia was able to see her sons use their father's hunting equipment and even wear some of his clothing with no problems at all. Lou burst into tears whenever she saw her husband's Bible. These decisions should be postponed for the most part, however, until the surety of a rational mind is achieved.

Part of the problem with memories rests in attitudes toward God. If we are able to thank Him sincerely for the good years we have had, then the memories will be happy ones. If we insist on pouting like petulant children who have just had their toys taken away, then memories will be painful. We don't enjoy a book less because it was loaned to us by a friend, nor do we erase the memories of a summer vacation because it was in a borrowed cottage or because it was of a limited duration.

Our relationship is with God, with the Giver and not the gift, the One who has already determined the perfect plan for our lives. Accepting God's plan for our lives means that we will enjoy the yesterdays as well as the todays and the tomorrows. The photograph album will be as great a source of pleasure to the widow as it was to the wife, and memories of days gone by will bring smiles instead of tears.

Not Ready to Walk Alone

TEARFUL memories are often caused by loneliness. The undying love, faithfulness, and assistance promised to the widow at the funeral last about one month. Dinner invitations quickly dwindle from the rush of calories that seriously threaten an entire wardrobe to vague remarks about "some night when Harry isn't home." The promise of "anything I can do" quickly turns into "the only night I can get into the gym—you understand." "If I can ever help with the kids" becomes "any other night" more rapidly than the approach of a Chicago snowstorm.

Loneliness travels under many guises, and delights in bursting full force upon its unsuspecting victim. Even before the funeral is over, the widow finds herself "saving up" conversations. "I can hardly wait to tell Jack that Art Jones was here" flashes through the widow's mind, and before the smile has had time to reach her face, she remembers that Jack isn't there to tell anymore. The habits formed over the years are not easily forgotten, but consolation comes with the realization that this type of loneliness passes away with time.

There is another kind of loneliness, best described as a state of mind. Not long after the funeral the widow realizes that while many people are interested in Suzy's "D" in math, and are even willing to offer much "helpful advice," some don't even smile when Suzy gets an "A+" in reading.

Acquaintances double over in laughter as you describe the harrowing time you had finding that little shop on the east side that specializes in needlepoint patterns, but few are willing to appreciate the victory involved in the fact that you were brave enough to look for it, and even drove on the expressway for the first time to do so.

Special friends help, but special friends usually have husbands and families who need and deserve their attention. We would be poor friends, indeed, if we insisted that they give ear to all of our conversational appetites.

THE secret of victory is outreach. Find a purpose in life outside of yourself. "Give, and it shall be given unto you; good measure, pressed down, and shaken together, and running over, shall men give into your bosom. For with the same measure that ye mete withal it shall be measured to you again" (Luke 6:38). As you fill the loneliness of others, your own loneliness disappears. This is not to say that we go looking for someone on whose shoulder we can cry, but rather it is offering our own shoulder in an effort to heal the problems of others.

Rachel invited one of the unmarried women in her church who was only slightly younger than herself to dinner several times. As the two women visited, the younger woman began to trust her and soon poured forth a tale of frustration and insecurity. In talking the problems through from a scriptural standpoint, the woman gained insights that helped her to see herself in a right light. The friendship has been a lasting one, and they have rejoiced together at the new romantic interest in the young woman's life that has resulted, in part, from her newfound confidence.

Beth gave her time and attention to a woman who was married to a wife-beating alcoholic. The two women spent many hours each week together for several years, praying and discussing the problems that constantly plagued this unfortunate family. When the husband finally came to know the Lord, he stated that Beth's faithfulness and love to his wife was one of the major influences in his decision to follow Christ. The wife testified that if it hadn't been for Beth she would have lost courage and either left her husband or committed suicide.

Looking inward may well pinpoint the cause of loneliness, but finding the cause does not eliminate the need for a cure. The outward look at the needs of others provides a sense of purpose that all of the self-searching of a lifetime can never accomplish.

Alison used her time to care for foster babies. Her gentle spirit and loving nature provided precisely the right start in life for youngsters who would later be adopted into families. The sadness of giving up a baby to new parents was always tempered by the joy of receiving a new one. One woman was heard to remark, "I sure wish she would have taken my babies for the first few weeks. She takes the thinnest, squalliest, ugly babies and turns them into cherubs."

Psalm 84 has a lovely thought in the sixth verse: "Who passing through the valley of Baca [or tears] make it a well . . . " The days of widowhood can be made a refreshing well of encouragement for others. Alison and Beth and Rachel used the time afforded them by their "misfortune" in ways that had positive effects in the lives of others.

DECISIONS sometimes seem harder to make alone. "How should I invest the funds received from my inheritance?" "Are the children receiving proper discipline?" "Should I let Johnny take saxophone lessons?" "Is this new hair style attractive?" "Should I buy the blue coat or the green one?" All are decisions that are easier to make with an outside opinion, especially when one is accustomed to the loving judgments of a husband.

Some expert views are necessary. Investment of funds for maximum benefit is not a decision to be made over coffee with an equally uninformed friend. Discipline of children is likewise an area for the experts. Your pastor may be able to help you or recommend some good books by child-care experts. A neighbor is usually the worst source of such information, and the conflicting opinions of various neighbors can do nothing but confuse the issue anyway.

Some decisions present a challenge to personal growth. Carol had worn the same hair style for more than ten years at her husband's request. The elegant, intricate twist had fitted his image of her as a cool sophisticate. His image was false, however; and as the lengths of hair fell to the beauty shop floor, Carol felt as if all the false trappings of the years fell away with them. Had she listened to all the plaintive cries of, "Not all that beautiful hair!" she might never have discovered herself as an individual. She didn't resent the years that she had pleased her husband instead of herself, but merely took advantage of the opportunity that was present.

THERE is one kind of loneliness which comes from too much company. In a two-parent family the children are a responsibility shared. The widowed mother bears the burden alone. All day, every day she is the figure of authority. There is no father to take over discipline, or to take the kids for a ride on Saturday afternoon, for that matter. There is no dad to play "horsey-back" in the yard while mom finishes those letters. Few things provoke the pain of jealousy more easily than for a widow who has just had a tiring day to view the neighbor romping with his children on the lawn while his wife is inside getting ready for the two of them to go out to dinner.

One person less doesn't make a lot of difference in the amount of work to be done. Clothes still need to be washed, floors still need to be scrubbed, and little ears get just as dirty without a father as they do with. Fatigue and self-pity go hand in hand, and often a good night's rest is all that is necessary to stamp out this form of loneliness.

The "big brother" or "big sister" concept can be as big a boon to the mother as to the children. Weekends with grandparents often accomplish more than just good relationships between them and the children; they also give mom time to be alone with her thoughts.

When such solutions aren't possible, mom should feel no guilt in hiring a babysitter for an afternoon so she can "regather her equilibrium." A little goes a long way, and frequently one afternoon will put a bright new outlook on several months. One week at summer camp for the children can change the course of an entire year.

THE loneliest people in the world are often found in crowds. The antithesis of loneliness is belonging, and the realization that she doesn't "belong" to anybody in the room sometimes leaves the widow moving for a time in a world that seems less than real. The Christian belongs, in a very real sense, to God, but it is earthly relationships that are considered important here. The antidote is simple—talk to somebody— quick!

Jan experienced the feeling for the first time one night after prayer meeting. Fortunately, the superintendent of the department in which she taught Sunday school had a question for her which brought her back to reality. The feeling didn't occur often, but when it did she was quick to talk to the person nearest her.

God has given each of us a will that is stronger than our emotions, and it is up to us to exercise that will to help ourselves over the difficult times. Most of us demonstrate the principle when we get up every morning. Seldom do we *feel* like getting up from a warm bed into a cold room. but the rewards of getting up far exceed those of staying in bed all day, and so we will ourselves to the proper action. We have this same power to will in every other situation where our emotions would seek to rule.

God has promised, ". . . I will never leave thee, nor forsake thee" (Heb. 13:5). For the widow who is walking in right relationship to Christ, this promise holds abundance of blessing. Not only is God an ever-present reality in daily life, but on those days that are the traditional stumbling blocks of widowhood there is comfort beyond all expectation . . .

> . . . at Christmas, as we joy in quiet meditation on the significance of Christ's birth,
> . . . at Easter, as we enjoy fellowship and share in the victory of a risen Savior,
> . . . on the anniversary of the death of our husbands, as we rejoice in the sufficiency of Christ for all our needs.

Pam dreaded the first anniversary of her husband's death,

and prayed that somehow she would be spared the emotionalism she was so prone to. Early in the morning she was awakened abruptly when the cat jumped onto her bed. She had overslept by thirty minutes and the animal was alerting her to the fact that breakfast was due. Getting her two children off to school on time proved to be the challenge of the morning, and she was glad to relax with a quiet cup of coffee as soon as they departed. Her relaxation was quickly ended when the phone rang. An out-of-town friend was in town and looking for an opportunity to chat and shop. By the time Pam had dressed, straightened the house, and made plans for dinner that evening, her friend was at the door. It wasn't until she noticed the date on her Bible-reading schedule that evening that she realized "the day" had gone by without notice. There were no tears, but much gratitude. God had simply filled every available moment. All "deliverances" are not quite that dramatic, but God is capable and willing to take care of every emotional need.

The Book of Hebrews tells us that Christ was "in all points tempted like as we are. . . ." (4:15) He has shared in everything that we have experienced, and He understands completely how we feel. No, He never lost a mate, but His loneliness far exceeded anything we can ever know. In the garden, deserted by friends, at the cross, abandoned by God, He reached depths of aloneness that our frail human minds can never comprehend.

Certainly, He will never leave us nor forsake us, and His constant, abiding presence will provide the comfort we need in the face of our loneliness. As we seek His face in the quiet moments alone, as we follow the example of Christ on earth seeking fellowship with His Father in prayer, we will find our greatest fulfillment and the peace that passes all understanding.

TV or Not TV

CHAPTER EIGHT

TV or Not TV

Loneliness is often spelled b-o-r-e-d-o-m. Lack of money or imagination or both sometimes limit the widow's entertainment to a variety of television shows and library books, neither of which is appealing as a steady diet. Should the TV shows be in bad taste one night (and many of them are), or should the book prove dull, the widow is left with nothing but four empty walls at which to stare. Or is she?

Singles clubs are often the first thought of the woman who has to readjust to the unmarried state. For the widow these are often disappointing, at best. Jenny's experience was a disaster. Attractive, under forty, and fun-loving, she attracted the unwelcome attention of two divorced men in her group. She got a little more adult companionship than she bargained for when the competition between the two men for her attention caused one of them to force his affections on her one evening.

Marilyn's story is not as disastrous as Jenny's, but it resulted in disillusionment just the same. Every meeting was filled with talk of visitation rights, alimony payments, remarriage for ex-mates, and all of the other ailments incumbent to divorced parties. While there are some similarities between widowed and divorced parents, the differences at times seem more outstanding. Often the widow finds that she has precious little fellowship with these people. Having no bitterness to dispel, no axe to grind, the venting of negative attitudes is depressing and offers little of interest.

Entertaining and being entertained become problems for some widows. Clare was distressed over the decrease in dinner invitations, until she realized that, out of embarrassment for her friends' husbands, she hadn't returned any of the invitations she had accepted. She reasoned that it was not much more trouble to entertain two or three couples at a time than one, and began inviting her friends in larger groups. The menu was sometimes not quite as elegant as if she were preparing for fewer people, but friendships were renewed and maintained. In relatively few weeks she found herself "back in the mainstream."

Fran decided that she liked entertaining smaller groups best, and really preferred having just one couple in for an evening. Proceeding on the theory that "if you feel like a fifth wheel, you'll probably act like one," she concentrated on cultivating meaningful conversation that would not be classified as "women's small talk." She knew political issues, was aware of current news reports, and even familiarized herself with some sports events in order to carry on intelligent conversations with either gender. Many a man was pleasantly surprised to discover that not only was she familiar with the names and positions of many football players, but was also able to discuss, with some degree of enthusiasm, the plays they had made in the previous week's game. The bonus for her was that she actually began to enjoy the sport! Several of her friends admitted that her approach had challenged them to follow her example so that they could talk more intelligently to their own husbands.

Limited budgets should only alter the type of entertaining one undertakes, not eliminate it. The friends, not the fare, are the issue. Spaghetti should be no less acceptable than steak. Hamburger stroganoff or sweet-sour chicken may be ultimately more satisfying than "pheasant en creme" or shrimp curry, as the competition for elegance of menu is eliminated.

SHIFTING of friends is inevitable to some degree. The transition of relating to singles is difficult for some couples. Joe and Mary could never understand why it might be difficult for Lucy to see them patting and petting each other throughout an evening. Dick and Roberta took the opposite approach and avoided each other to the point that their widowed friend was uncomfortable. Knowing that she was the source of the coolness between them only amplified the problem.

Some couples are friends primarily for the husbands' sake. Dave and Fred had hunted, fished, bowled, and repaired their automobiles together for years. It was natural that they would entertain each other in their homes, wives included. The two wives, however, had little to share. Dave's wife was totally committed to helping her husband's rapidly expanding business to succeed, and Fred's wife had as her main interest the care of their two small children. When Fred died, Dave and his wife made an effort to invite the young widow to their home, but the two women had so little in common that the effort was futile.

New friendships will form. In the previous chapter on loneliness we talked about widows who had befriended some of the never-married women in the church. The friendships thus

formed often provide more than just "somebody to talk to."
Here is the companion for concerts and plays. Here is the
someone who may be willing (and probably as eagerly as the
widow) to visit the "nice" restaurant.

The time the widow spends with her children should also
be classed as entertainment. Children are delightful individuals, and getting to know them is one of the satisfactions of
parenthood. In addition to the usual games and shopping
excursions, there are multitudes of things to do.

Rare is the city or town that does not have some interesting manufacturing operation to observe nearby. Usually,
within an hour's drive, there is some maker of shoes, salad
dressing, soda pop, chocolate chips, or automobiles. Many of
these manufacturers conduct scheduled tours. One young
mother and her children were so intrigued by a candy factory
that they toured the establishment twice in one summer.
Quaint historical villages have sprung up throughout the na-
tion in recent years, and ethnic groups sponsor many "settlements" for touring purposes.

Sally and her children enjoyed the zoo and museum in
their city. Their frequent excursions provided many pleasant
afternoons of entertainment at minimal cost. Joan and her
husband had enjoyed camping with the children before his
death. Being an adventurous individual, Joan continued the
activity with her children. Penny outdid her, however. Always
interested in camping but having no experience with it, she
consulted some friends who had camped often and were able to
give valuable advice as to necessary equipment and safety
precautions. She and her children camped for the first time
with borrowed equipment, but soon repeated the experience
with their own, as camping became regular family vacation
fare.

Children, too, enjoy restaurants. Parents often treat their
offspring to "Toodles McDoodles" hamburgers, but quite frequently hire a babysitter for anything more elegant.
Candlelight and flocked wallpaper may be the extreme, but an

occasional treat to a "real restaurant" will not only make your children feel more important, but will also prepare them for social contacts they will make in years to come.

Travel is not prohibitively difficult for women. Tours offered through local travel agencies and social groups are often delightful. Hazel and her widowed sister-in-law scanned the offerings regularly and planned and saved for at least two trips per year. Beverly and her friend decided that an automobile was the only way to travel with children. The single friend helped to care for the three youngsters and shared lodging expenses. They cooked their meals "camp style" to save money and to allow the children time to exercise and burn off excess energy. They so enjoyed the trip westward to the national parks that they are now planning a similar vacation in the South.

IF RECREATION means only entertaining and being entertained, then the widow might well complain of boredom. Even the well-provided-for woman will want to limit the amount of traveling she does. Dinner out or guests in are fine in moderation, but few waistlines or dispositions can stand a steady procession of such fare.

To those who seek their recreation in relating to others, the possibilities are exciting. Gwen became involved with the Ladies' Missionary Society in her church more fully than she was able to when her husband was alive. Her work brought her into close contact with the missionaries supported by the church budget; and being informed about their needs and ministries, she was able to carry on an effective prayer ministry. She encouraged others to pray, also, and often within weeks or days they would hear of God's answers to their prayers. When one missionary was to have emergency surgery for suspected cancer, the need was met before the request could be published.

Kay's Sunday school class of fifth-grade girls was delighted when they were invited to picnics, slumber parties, and

Saturday-afternoon get-togethers. Each of the seven girls was invited individually to dinner at her teacher's house, and each was visited in her own home at least twice during the year. Few of those girls will ever forget her. Two of them will remember eternally that it was her concerned time and effort that brought them to a saving knowledge of Jesus Christ.

Seldom do the church shut-ins receive enough company. Shirley sought to fill part of the gap, and each week would visit three or four of those who were no longer able to get out of their homes. She often brought a simple gift: a scented bar of soap, a pretty candle, a handkerchief, a plate of home-baked cookies (for those whose health did not prevent such gifts of food). Her thoughtfulness was amply rewarded as these senior citizens shared the riches of a lifetime of walking with Christ. Often she left their homes feeling as if she, not they, had been ministered to.

Another kind of "shut-in" who is often ignored is the young mother who is kept home with the responsibility of preschool children. These women often hunger for companionship, and an afternoon chat could change the course of an entire week for one of them. Sue offered to babysit, free of charge, for an afternoon a week for one such mother. The afternoon of shopping, or just getting away for lunch with a friend without the responsibility of children, helped change that mother's entire attitude of sad-faced boredom to happy acceptance of her role.

Letting your pastor know what jobs you are capable of and willing to do often presents opportunities for service. Knowing that Carla had been trained as a teacher and that she was willing to help in any way enabled her pastor to pair her with a junior-high girl who was having difficulty with her studies. Carla's ability to work with teens helped tutor the girl through a difficult year, and helped her gain a positive attitude about herself which was reflected in all of her future studies.

Sharon's willingness to use her past secretarial training enabled her to help the church secretary through especially busy times. In typing envelopes, filing nonconfidential material, and phone-answering she freed the secretary's time for more urgent matters.

Betty's organizational abilities were exactly fitting to the needs of the church's music minister. Her work put the entire music program in order for the first time in years. The scramble to find sufficient copies of music for the entire choir was eliminated with her orderly filing system, and the damage often caused by careless searching was reduced to a minimum.

When a couple from Vietnam arrived in her neighborhood, with three small children, Alice made herself available to teach the somewhat timid young wife the English language. Since Alice did not speak Vietnamese and the woman spoke no English, the project was a challenging one. It was eventually rewarded by an opportunity to tell her new friend about the love of Jesus Christ and the meaning of His death. The love that these two women shared for each other was reflected in the attitudes of three young Vietnamese children who ran to "Auntie Alice" with smiling faces and uplifted arms each time they saw her.

Joan was burdened for the salvation of the deaf couple in her neighborhood. When sign-language classes were offered in the city's adult education program, she was the first to sign up. A subsequent Bible study in the home of the deaf couple led to the salvation of both husband and wife and several of their deaf friends.

Jane volunteered to teach discipleship classes for newly converted women. Often these women were still in the midst of family criticism and disapproval over their conversions, and Jane's encouragement and prayers kept many of them from despair. When the women began to see those in their families come to faith, Jane's reward in joy seemed far greater than any warranted by the effort she had spent in preparing for the classes.

HOME Bible studies are an effective evangelistic tool. They do require organization, however, and often the widow is the person who has the time to do this. Materials can be found in many Christian bookstores. Christian magazines usually list several studies that can be ordered, and often a pastor is willing and able to help locate the necessary basics as well as giving guidance for the conduct of the studies. There are few thrills equal to seeing neighborhood women come to know Christ through Bible study and then watching them grow spiritually through the same program. As these women are directed into the local church, and then as their families are reached for Christ, the effects of such a ministry are far-reaching.

Shirley didn't feel capable of tutoring or teaching or leading a Bible study group, but a sincere desire to minister to others led her to investigate the needs of out-of-town college students and servicemen. She began a letter-writing ministry that blessed all who were recipients of it. She wrote to each student and serviceman from the church on a monthly basis, keeping them informed of church events within their own age groups, and often enclosed the church bulletins. She made it clear that a reply was not necessary because she was fully aware of the demands on their time. Her letters were so welcome, however, that her mailbox was often jammed with replies. Never "gossipy," her ministry of love brought home a little closer for many.

Marcia wrote to the missionaries supported by her church. She too made it clear that replies were not necessary, realizing that there were pressures on their time and energy. Her concern for the welfare of these missionaries was so evident that they made sure that she was kept abreast of developments on the field. Many reasoned that if she was concerned enough to write and not demand their time, she was concerned enough to pray.

SOMETIMES reaching out to others requires more training than a widow has in her background. Barbara had begun teacher training before her marriage, and when her husband died she returned to complete the work for her degree. Sue decided to take secretarial training at a Bible college. Both found that the years they spent studying were some of the most fulfilling they had known as they were faced with new ideas, met new people, and learned the skills necessary to assist them after graduation.

Shelley didn't feel that she was capable of full-time college work, and the nearest Bible college was several hundred miles away, so part-time attendance was impossible. She availed herself of correspondence courses however, and the teacher training she received through them, along with the Bible courses she was able to take, transformed her into one of the best teachers in her church's Sunday school. Before long she was sharing her newly acquired knowledge and skills with others, and the effect was felt throughout the church in increased interest in the Sunday school program.

Recreation depends more on definition than on specific activity. As we reach out to meet the needs of others, our own needs will be met. Human need is the most abundant commodity on earth. The poor will always need clothing, the lonely will always need comfort, the young will always need example and teaching. As we sew or visit or teach, we will experience not just the passing flight of fancy, ever seeking new and greater diversions, but we will know the deep and abiding joy that comes from knowing we have truly helped another. The complaint of the person truly interested in helping others will never be that of boredom. Rather, the constant plea will be for more hours to help meet the needs that are seen.

CHAPTER NINE.

Nobody Touches
Me Any More

Nobody Touches Me Any More

Physically, the first reaction of the widow is numbness. Possibly the furthest thought from her mind is that she will ever again experience desire for a man. Those feelings return however, surprisingly soon, especially if she had a satisfactory relationship with her husband.

The widow sometimes responds to the return of her sexual appetite with shock and guilt. The unwelcome dreams and unexpected desires become an embarrassment, and many a woman has accused herself of being sinful because of them. Certainly they are not sinful. They are the natural result of a life lived together by a man and a woman in the way God intended for them to live. Any sin involved lies not in the remembrance of marital pleasure, but only in dwelling on it until it becomes frustrating desire.

Call it the "Hot Fudge Principle." Imagine for a moment that you're hungry—not steak hungry, but just enough to want something that's not on the diet you started this morning. Now picture a hot fudge sundae. The ice cream is cold and creamy. The fudge is really hot, not that tepid, thick, grainy blob of chocolate that some dump sparingly over ice milk infested with watery chips of hardness, but smooth and rich and dark, melting the ice cream it touches. Even the whipped cream is perfect—light, with just enough to garnish without drowning the whole creation. The nuts aren't just ground-up peanuts, either, but pecan halves—and they're salted—and the cherry isn't just a little sliver, but whole, just the way you like them.

If you concentrate on that sundae for very long, and think about its pleasurable qualities, and then think about the fact that you're slightly hungry, the chances are that you're going to start wanting a hot fudge sundae. Now imagine that you've been told that you may never have another hot fudge sundae as long as you live. The probabilities are good that you can work yourself into quite a frenzy over hot fudge sundaes.

The same thing happens with sexual desires. If we dwell on our lack of fulfillment and the fact that such lack is through no fault of our own, then we are adding to our own problems. The desires will come, but we must learn not to fix our thoughts on them. Paul gives the perfect answer in Philippians 4:8: "Finally, brethren, whatsoever things are true, whatsoever things are honest, whatsoever things are just, whatsoever things are pure, whatsoever things are lovely, whatsoever things are of good report; if there be any virtue, and if there be any praise, think on these things."

The world, the flesh, and the devil cannot win over the power of God's Word. If your Bible is at hand, read it, and *concentrate* on what it is saying. If it is not near, then concentrate on the Word you have memorized. Willfully push the thoughts out of your mind, and they will not be able to rule over you. Here is one of the few problem areas in life where a woman can realistically say, "Ignore it, and it will go away!"

TEMPTATION in the realm of physical desires will come, whether it be in the mind or in physical reality. A flirtation, the smell of aftershave lotion, a familiar action that triggers a response are all appeals to the flesh. Remember David. He was tempted by the sight of Bathsheba's body and yielded to that temptation. The rest of his life (and Israel's history) bore the scars of that sin (2 Sam. 11–12). The child born as a result of his weakness died, and his family was divided and lived continually under the threat of the sword.

Whatever the temporary satisfactions of illicit sexual relations, the price is far too high. The aftershave lotion may smell headily sweet, but the smell of guilt is stench. The warmth of strong arms may be the most delightful thought imaginable, but loss of fellowship with God because of sin is a loneliness no man can ever fill. The temptation of a forbidden kiss may make your heart swell into your throat, but the memory of the results of that forbidden moment may well sting for a lifetime.

To toy with adultery, fornication, or any other form of sexual satisfaction is to disobey God. Scripture condones no other outlet for sexual desires than the marriage bed; anything else places one in far greater jeopardy of unhappiness than was ever imagined at the first.

God does not mock the widow. He does not give her desires and then laugh at her frustration when those desires must go unfilled. Identification of the underlying causes of the feelings that seem most obvious often reduces the problem to manageable limits.

Marital sex is associated with affection and acceptance, and in a moment of loneliness those feelings can easily be misinterpreted as sexual desire. The more useful a woman becomes—the busier she is in meeting the needs of others— the less will be her own need. The Sunday school teacher who has a half-dozen young girls clamoring for her attention has little problem feeling accepted or loved. The woman who has just led someone from their problems to the solution of a Christ-centered life may have trouble falling asleep at night because of excitement, but affection and acceptance will not trouble her.

Touch is another important part of marital communication that is often an underlying cause of frustration. The quick hug, the "peck on the cheek," the touch of a hand are all means of saying much without saying anything. Rather than mourn their loss, we can learn their importance and then use that knowledge in the encouragement of others. Again, we bring to mind the Sunday school class. The confidence of the neglected or insecure child can be raised to new levels by the simple means of that same quick hug or by resting a hand on his shoulder as you talk to him. Touch communicates love, and if we concentrate on giving, rather than receiving, we can bring new joy and meaning into the lives of others who might otherwise never know.

When physical desires become a problem, many a woman does well to look at her calendar. "This too shall pass away" is a motto that can still many a storm. During ovulation and in the days immediately before and after her menstral period, a woman's desires are at their peak. To be aware that a situation is only temporary is often knowledge that brings victory.

Finally, prayer brings victory. As we seek our Father's face and ask for His help in time of temptation, He is more than willing to help. We are told, "There hath no temptation taken you but such as is common to man: but God is faithful, who will not suffer you to be tempted above that ye are able; but will with the temptation also make a way to escape, that ye may be able to bear it" (1 Cor. 10:13). Again the answer is attitude. If we choose to make this area of our lives a major concern, then it will obligingly become so. But if we focus on God and on His perfect plan for our lives, victory is already assured.

GOD created you as a woman. Unfortunately, some women forget that fact when they become widows. Their clothes, their hair, and their countenances become as drab as November grass. They seem to think that because their husbands are gone there is no more reason to be attractive. Appearances are important. God may look upon the heart, but people can only see the outside, and they often judge the inner condition by the outer appearance.

Less than three weeks after the death of her husband of nearly forty years, Vivian appeared in church with a salon hair style, a new cherry-colored coat, and a smile on her face. Nobody judged her as brazen, and many were encouraged by her spirit of joy and faith in God.

The younger widow would do well to take heed. We would not encourage any false pretense or superficial attitudes, and certainly not disregard propriety, but stringy hair proves nothing except the need for a shampoo. A new wardrobe at this time is out of place, and perhaps a drastic change in hair-color would best wait awhile, but bright colors and a smile almost always have a place.

In addition to the encouragement of others, self-image is important. As the object of God's special love and care, we are to have a proper concept of our worth as individuals. Because a mate has died does not mean that we are worth less than we were before, and it doesn't help to build proper self-images when all we see in the mirror is a gray face matched by equally gray apparel. Such attitudes say only, "I don't care about God's love. It isn't enough for me."

Some of a woman's femininity lies in contrast. When the male side of that contrast is gone, quite a few women find that their tastes change somewhat. If additional ruffles and lace or pretty nightgowns and/or robes help to make up the difference, even if nobody sees them except yourself, there is sufficient reason for their purchase. Regular visits to the hairdresser are a morale boost that are often worth far more than the price paid. No woman need feel that she is squandering money on such things unless such expenditure is really a serious drain on the family budget.

Often it is a very small thing that makes up the difference. Dora bought flowered bedsheets, something she would never have considered while her husband was alive. Sliding between blue daisies each night made her feel delightfully feminine, and the lilac-scented talc which she had sprinkled between the sheets reminded her of that femininity long after the lights had been turned out.

Joy, whose taste frequently had run to the austere, suddenly began to paint her toenails pink after her husband passed away. Except in summer sandals, no one ever knew but herself. It did wonders for her self-concept.

TO MANY, remarriage is considered the ideal solution for loneliness, sexual problems, and financial difficulties. Like unhappy teenagers running away from an unpleasant home situation, they eagerly grasp at the first proposal that comes their way. In addition to the usual dangers present in such a hasty decision, there are several more for the widow to consider about which the first-time bride need not concern herself. The immaturity and self-centeredness that see marriage as a method of problem solving lead also to the new set of difficulties inherent in the proposed solution.

The woman who seeks marriage to solve her problems may constantly contend with the tendency to compare. In every difficult situation she will look to the past. Combined with the tendency to eulogy, there is scarcely a man alive who will survive psychologically. Accusations need not be made in so many words. If "John was always kind, considerate, and picked up his shoes," then Harry will interpret every sigh or discontented murmur while his wife is picking up his shoes (or his dirty socks or his newspaper) to mean that he is not kind or considerate.

The same inflexibility that plagues her single life will plague the woman who marries as an escape from that life, and probably to a greater degree. If a widow can't readjust to living with herself, she certainly can't be expected to readjust to living with another person. If the widow or her prospective mate has children, the problem will be compounded. The multiple adjustments that must be made require maturity and flexibility, not the self-minded desire to be rid of existing problems.

Eileen was only twenty-eight when her husband was killed in an automobile accident. Unable to cope with loneliness and the responsibilities of three small children, she accepted the marriage proposal of a policemen acquaintance of her husband less than eight months after she became a widow. Two weeks after the wedding he was arrested for immoral conduct, lost his job, and was forced to take his new family out of the city to escape the stigma of the charge against him. Removed from every source of security she had in relatives and family friends, life became miserable for Eileen. "Marry in haste, repent at leisure" is a moral not just for young girls. The more experienced need also to heed its wisdom.

Remarriage is by no means slated for failure, nor is early remarriage to be considered less than honorable. The caution is merely to examine motive. Marriage is never an "escape." Rather, at any age, a couple should be willing to ask themselves whether they are more effective for Christ together than they are apart. Unless that question can be answered in the affirmative, they would do best to go their separate ways. People wrapped up in the solving of their own problems cannot be effective in solving the problems of others.

One remarried-widower missionary wrote, as he visited the field where his wife and her first husband had served the Lord, "Today I sat at his desk, ate at his table, and slept in his bed. What a joy it was to think of the years that they served the Lord together here." The Christ-honoring union of these two families should not be the exception but rather the standard for Christian attitudes toward remarriage.

Not Ready to Walk Alone

IN CONTRAST to those who seek matrimonial bonds too soon or for the wrong reasons, there are those who sweetly proclaim, "There was only one Joe, and since I'll never find another like him, I'll never remarry." This attitude says many things, and some of them are not as complimentary as one would first imagine.

Those who live in a state of perpetual mourning do their mates no honor. Rather, remarriage is the highest praise one can pay to a deceased mate. It says, in effect, "Marriage is good, and I want to be part of that good relationship again." To reject any possibility of another union may well be saying some telling things about the first one. It certainly projects a negative self-image as it declares a selfish unwillingness to adjust to living with another person. At the same time, it says some unkind things about the deceased husband. In order to be married to such a person, he certainly settled for what was less than the best.

Such an attitude also denies the power of God. If God was able to bring into one's life a mate with which a happy marriage was achieved, then He certainly is able to repeat the performance. He may not always do so, but the possibilities are as unlimited as God Himself.

All the world loves a lover, and half of it becomes downright giddy if they are responsible for introducing two people who eventually marry. If one of the parties to be introduced happens to be a widow or a widower, some normal, well-adjusted individuals who are capable of holding jobs, raising children, and paying their bills on time seemingly lose complete control of their senses.

Matchmaking friends become, alternately, trials to the widow's patience, providers of humorous anecdotes, thorns in the flesh, and people who genuinely allow God to work through them.

The Bible clearly states that the widow is "at liberty to be married to whom she will; only in the Lord" (1 Cor. 7:39). The nominal Christianity of some potential husbands introduced by "friends" to the widow is shocking. Additionally, divorced persons are introduced despite the attendant problems in such a union.[1] One pastor even suggested such an introduction to a mission-bound widow in his congregation, despite the fact that any marriage to a divorced person would disqualify her from service with most mission boards! To some persons, the only qualification for a match is a state of singleness, and it is these that become thorns in the flesh of the widow.

There is one Matchmaker, however, that no widow need fear. Ever since creation He has been pairing couples successfully, beginning with Adam and Eve, extending through Abraham and Sarah, Isaac and Rebekah, Jacob and Rachel, and on to Mary and Joseph. For the widow Ruth He found Boaz, and for Abigail He found David.[2]

Some biblical widows remained unmarried, however. There is no record that the widow of Zarepheth ever remarried, nor the widow of Nain. Perhaps the most outstanding widow is Anna, who spent her entire life, after seven years of marriage, in fasting and prayer. Her reward for such service was to see and recognize the infant Messiah.[3]

Remarriage for the widow is optional, according to Scripture. How well the widow would do to leave that option with the Lord. To remarry hastily, and/or to wed someone who is not God's choice, is by far worse than to remain in an unmarried state.

The story is told of a Russian man who dearly loved his wife of many years. Upon her death he became desperately lonely and nightly demanded of God, "God, give me a wife." Shortly thereafter he met a widow of about his own age and

---

[1]While some teach that remarriage of divorced persons is not a scriptural practice, others disagree with this view. For a discussion of the latter concept, see John Murray, *Divorce* (Nutley, N.J.: Presbyterian and Reformed Publishing Co., 1953).

[2]Accounts of these couples' lives may be found in these passages of Scripture: Genesis 2:18ff.; 12; 24; 29ff.; Matthew 1; Luke 1; Ruth; 1 Samuel 24.

[3]Biblical accounts of these women's lives may be found as follows: 1 Kings 17; Luke 7:11ff.; 2:36ff.

married her. Within the year his life was torment, for he had wed a shrew. There was nothing he could do that would satisfy her demands for worldly goods; his habits did not please her; and his temperament was too bland to suit her. Day by day his countenance fell, as he realized that God had given him what he demanded, and now he would spend the rest of his life with the answer to that demand.

THE WIDOW is in a unique position. Having escaped the "stigma" of having never been married, she is free from the social pressure that is brought to bear on many single women. For the most part, she has probably also satisfied her desire for children. She is free, for the second time, to decide what course her life will take.

If a woman can leave that choice to God, trusting Him for either the single or the married life, she is truly the freest of all of His creation. In complete dependence upon God, she finds that she does not need to depend on an earthly relationship for her well-being. Should opportunity for remarriage occur, she has laid the base to present herself as a whole person, not one who is merely seeking the solution to personal problems. Her decision can be made without the hindering voice of emotionalism.

Whether she decides to remarry or not, the widow who has committed her life to God has learned through her experience that her fellowship is with One who will not get moody and out of sorts, her Provider is One who owns the cattle on a thousand hills, her Comforter is One who truly understands because He has shared her infirmity, and her Beloved is none other than the great I Am.